Crowded House

COMPLETE

THE BIOGRAPHY

THE DISCOGRAPHY

THE LYRICS

THE MUSIC

THE INDEX

CONTENTS

IMP

International
MUSIC
Publications

International Music Publications Limited
Griffin House 161 Hammersmith Road London W6 8BS England

This book © 1999 International Music Publications Limited
ISBN: 1–85909 625–5
Order Ref: 6223A

Distributed by:
International Music Publications Limited
Griffin House, 161 Hammersmith Road, London W6 8BS

International Music Publications Germany
Marstallstrasse 8, D-80539 München, Germany

Danmusik
Vognmagergade 7, DK1120 Cioenhage K, Denmark

Nuova Carisch Srl.
Via Campania, 12, 20098 San Giuliano Milanese, Milano, Italy

Carisch France, SARL
20, rue de la Ville-l'Eveque, 75008 Paris, France

Nueva Carisch Espana S.L.
Via Magallenes 25, 28015 Madrid, Spain

Warner/Chappell Music Inc, Australia
1 Cassius Avenue, North Sydney, New South Wales 2060, Australia

Warner/Chappell Notservice AB
PO Box 533, Vendevagen 85 B, S-182 15 Danderyd, Sweden

Music transcribed and processed by
Barnes Music Engraving Limited
East Sussex TN22 4HA

Cover design by xheight design limited

Reproduced and printed by
Halstan & Co. Ltd., Amersham, Bucks., England

Many thanks to Grant Thomas Management for their help throughout the
production of this book – it has been greatly appreciated.

the BIOGRAPHY

BIOGRAPHY

"The way we make mistakes together gives us a distinct sound. I think a good band is a product of the members having different perspectives and the blend being kind of out-of-shape, but distinctive."
(Neil Finn)

The music of Crowded House is more than distinctive. Some songs you'll remember intimately – *Don't Dream It's Over* and *Weather With You* have passed into folk memory. That's expected. It'll be the others that catch you off guard. The way *Four Seasons In One Day* injects fresh foreboding into the air like an oncoming storm; the unmistakable way that *Distant Sun* has of identifying itself with a chorus you could gladly mistake for an old friend. It's the thing that Crowded House do best – slipping beneath your skin bearing all the hallmarks of Great Pop , so that before you can find out if the symptoms are normal, your mind's already made up. Crowded House, you see, are the nearest you'll get to a musical truth drug.

Hard Times

After the break up of influential New Zealand group, Split Enz, in 1984, former members Neil Finn and Paul Hester recruited Craig Hooper (former member of Australian group The Reels) as second guitarist and Nick Seymour (brother of Hunters & Collectors' lead singer Mark) as bassist. Two years later, the band who had named themselves the Mullanes, after Finn's mother's maiden name, signed to Capitol Records in Los Angeles on the strength of a demo tape and their previous track-record with the Enz.

The signing with Capitol brought about some significant changes; firstly, the Mullanes were re-named Crowded House, after the somewhat squashed Hollywood home that the band shared with their families. Then came the departure of Hooper, who quit the group and returned to his old band, The Reels; followed by the arrival of Mitchell Froom, who was brought in to produce their debut LP.

Unfortunately, these changes did not bring about immediate success. Crowded House's debut and self-titled album was released in August 1986 to little fanfare. The critical acclaim was better – of great interest to collectors even now, is the fact that the track listing differs depending on the album's country of origin. Every release contained ten tracks, (except for the British CD which contained all eleven), but side two of the Australian edition featured *Can't Carry On*, while the UK issue included a new version of *I Walk Away*, a track which originally appeared on the last Split Enz LP **See Ya Round**. Following that, despite reaching No 45 in the UK charts, and earning a multi-format release, the band's first single, *World Where You Live*, also did not earn the commercial response desperately needed by the band. Once again however, the song about a neurotic contemplating who or what his lover is thinking about during sex, became a collectors item, as one of the UK's first CD singles.

Recognition

It was only a year later that the band had its first worldwide hit with *Don't Dream It's Over*. Chart success was not instant though; the single was released three times in the UK, and the band spent much of the last part of 1986 doing low-key acoustic performances in restaurants in both Europe and America. Only a while later, when American radio stations suddenly started playing the single, did interest generate. Certain people were surprised – bands don't usually get to No 2 in America by writing abstract ballads about such simple emotions. But then, Crowded House and the rule book have never seen eye to eye, finding new ways to fuse rapture and regret with every new album.

By June 1987, the popularity of *Don't Dream It's Over* had spread over the Atlantic, and had reached the Top 30 in the UK charts. Meanwhile, the band was enjoying chart success with their second single, *Something So Strong*, which peaked at No 7 in July. Eventually, the debut album sold platinum in both America and Canada, triple platinum in New Zealand and quadruple platinum in Australia.

Throughout the first few months of 1988, Crowded House recorded their second album in Melbourne and Los Angeles. Morale was good after their recent successes, and so the album, **Temple Of Low Men** was released worldwide in July 1988. Another world tour kicked off in Europe, followed by a tour of Australia. However, the three month North American tour was cancelled as the album had failed to live up to commercial expectations in the USA, and reached only No 40. "To me it wasn't any more melancholy or down than the first album," explained Finn. "We tried to create more texture in the songs, and the image was enhanced by the fact that we weren't quite as willing to be those fun-loving guys from Down Under anymore."

The first single to be released from the LP, *Better Be Home Soon* flopped in the UK, and only reached No 42 in the US. *Sister Madly*, was equally unsuccessful. Despite featuring an impressive guitar solo by Richard Thompson, no new tracks were added; the flipside was lazily a King Biscuit Live Hour version of *Something So Strong*.

Homeward bound

And so the members of Crowded House returned to Australia, where their album was a success. They went on to record *Recurring Dream*, which was included on the soundtrack to the Mel Gibson/Michelle Pfeiffer film *Tequila Sunrise*, and mysteriously appeared as a B-side to the Australian single, *Now We're Getting Somewhere*. Years later it appeared on the Australian single of *It's Only Natural*.

Producing their next album, **Woodface**, turned out to be problematic. Neil Finn had problems coming up with ideas for new songs that reached his own expectations, and political problems within the band led to the departure of Nick Seymour. Meanwhile, Neil got together with his older brother and former Split Enz colleague Tim Finn, to write songs for a **Finn Brothers** duo album. Having never written together before, the brothers wrote fifteen songs in a two week period.

A short time later, Nick Seymour returned to the band, and in December 1989 Crowded House plus a temporarily reformed Split Enz did a brief tour of Australia. Neil Finn spent the first half of 1990 working on both the new Crowded House album and the **Finn Brothers** duo record. The decision was then made to combine the two LPs, and invite Tim Finn to join Crowded House as a permanent member.

"It was very difficult to separate them [LP's]," said Neil. "I thought it would be so much simpler if we were all together, and when Tim played some gigs with us as a fourth member it was fine." In June 1991, the **Woodface** album was finally released in all formats, including a picture disc CD. (A particular favourite is a limited edition American issue CD, as it is presented as an open-up pack, complete with a cut-away cover and pictures of the band.) A blend of the moodiness of **Temple Of Low Men** and the charm of **Crowded House**, it was recorded in Los Angeles again with Mitchell Froom. Receiving ecstatic reviews and selling over 1.2 million copies worldwide, **Woodface** went Top 20 in eight countries, peaking No 6 in the UK, No 2 in Australia and No 1 in New Zealand. The band toured for a solid eighteen months after the release of the album, during which time they were voted "Best Live Act" by the readership of the UK's Q Magazine. The tours included Crowded House's return to Britain later that year, and significantly, gigs at the Hammersmith Odeon, two nights at the Town & Country Club, plus most of their first gigs outside the capital were sold out. However, whilst touring, Tim left the band. Nick Seymour explained: "It wasn't working on stage. Tim was mainly playing keyboards so he couldn't focus on being lead singer, which is what he wanted to be." LA session player Mark Hart was quickly brought in, having previously toured with them during the **Temple** dates, and having played on the **Woodface** album.

Success

Meanwhile, after a rather disappointing response to *Chocolate Cake* (the first single released from **Woodface**), the group's profile was ironically being boosted by the huge UK success of the single *Fall At Your Feet*. Two separate singles were issued – the first coming in a fold-out wallet in which to insert the second! *Fall At Your Feet* included two live recordings – *Now We're Getting Somewhere* which was recorded at a gig in San Francisco, and an acoustic recording of *Six Months In A Leaky Boat*. Capitol was rather cheeky in their decision to include the second track – it previously appeared on Tim Finn's 1989 **How'm I Gonna Sleep**! Only previously released material was included on the second part of the double single package, but positive feedback from the fans pushed the single to the Top 20.

The success of the band continued to increase with a number of TV appearances, regular airplay and more UK performances. Crowded House finally made their breakthrough in April 1992, when their next single, *Weather With You*, reached No 6 in the UK charts. Despite a catchy, if a little tacky melody, Neil Finn attributed its success to timing rather than quality: "It seems almost irrelevant what the song was, it could have been any of five or six tracks. Not that I'm knocking it, it's obviously pretty catchy! But everything seems to have come together because we finally got the timing right. In England it seems that if you're not there in the right two weeks you might not as well be there at all: everything goes up and down so fast."

Musical genius

Eventually, after an extensive stretch of touring, TV appearances and mayhem, Crowded House needed to get away, head for the beach and make another album. So they went and did all three. The result was **Together Alone**, which made its European and Australasian release in October 1993. Having recorded their previous albums in Los Angeles, a beach called Kare Kare on the remote rugged west coast of Auckland, New Zealand was quite a change of scenery and pace. During the summer, they set up a studio which was walking distance from the sea. This rustic isolated spot, where the Tasman Sea pounds the beach underneath the bush-clad hills of the Waitakere Ranges, provided the influence for the album's first track, *Kare Kare*.

From this opening song to the closing title track, the album runs through a variety of congruous styles. There is the balladry of *Fingers Of Love*, which reached No 25 in the UK charts; the expansive pop of *In My Command*, the guitar grooves of *Black & White Boy* and *Locked Out*, and the widescreen stellar numbers of *Catherine Wheel* and *Private Universe*. The latter features the polyrhythmic percussion of a troupe of log drummers from Auckland's Island community, along with the Waka Huia Maori Choir and a brass band feature on the album's title and closing anthem *Together Alone*. Both tracks were recorded live in just one day. "We thought it would be great to get together all these elements that to us are evocative of the South Pacific without trying to be high-minded about it," comments Neil. "Just have fun with it and throw them together."

Aiding and abetting that process was English producer Youth, working on his first Crowded House album. The former Killing Joke bass player, now better known for his dance remixes and production skills, was perhaps an unlikely figure to produce the band's more careful recording tendencies and encourage them to experiment. And so the more rock-orientated American, Bob Clearmountain, who had contributed to the previous two albums, was brought in for the final mixes. Finn explained why: "Bob makes everything seem so simple. We were able to be very loose and uninhibited with what went on tape because we knew Bob would sort it out. His mixes sound huge."

Having reached No 5 in the UK, the album failed to earn commercial success in the US. The album's promotional tour included America, but on April 14 1994, two hours before a gig in Atlanta, Paul Hester informed the band that he would quit right after that gig, citing the pressures of touring and a declining motivation as his reasons. However, the ambience of the band's future gigs remained unchanged. "That's the only way we know how to do it", said Neil in 1988. "We're really flying on the seat of our pants whenever we play live, and I think the audience knows that. That's where the buzz comes in."

Epilogue

In June 1996, Crowded House completed their Capitol contract with the release of **Recurring Dream (The Very Best Of Crowded House)**. A synopsis of the band's ten year life, it combines those old favourites – *Weather With You* and *Don't Dream It's Over* – with some of the band's most memorable live appearances, improvised and otherwise. It includes four songs from every album, three new songs, and for speedy purchasers, a free live album. The old "crowd" gathered for the album, Mitchell Froom was brought in to produce it, while Paul Hester was invited to play drums on the new tracks. However, the album turned out to be the band's last. On Saturday November 23rd, 1996, Crowded House performed their farewell concert on the steps of the Sydney Opera House. They agreed to the farewell concert on two conditions; one that it would be absolutely free to the public, and two: that any funds raised would directly benefit the Sydney Children's Hospital, Randwick. The concert was a tremendous success – over 100,000 people attended. Neil Finn commented: "It seems important to have a ritual farewell for us as well as our audience." Songwriter Neil Finn is currently developing his solo career, and has already produced one solo album.

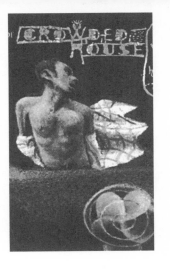

the DISCOGRAPHY

DISCOGRAPHY 1986-1996

Crowded House (EP)
Capitol EST 2016 (LP)/TCEST 2016 (Cassette)/CDP 7466932 (CD)
Released: April 1986
Titles: Mean To Me (Finn)/World Where You Live (Finn)/Now We're Getting Somewhere (Finn)/Don't Dream It's Over (Finn)/Love You 'Til The Day I Die (Finn)/Something So Strong (Finn, Froom)/Hole In The River (Finn, Rayner)/Can't Carry On (Finn)/I Walk Away (Finn)/Tombstone (Finn)/That's What I Call Love (Finn, Hester)

World Where You Live (Finn)/**That's What I Call Love** (Finn, Hester)
Capitol Records CL 416 (7")
Released: July 1986

World Where You Live (extended version) (Finn)/**Something So Strong** (Finn, Froom)/**Don't Dream It's Over** (Finn)/**That's What I Call Love** (Finn, Hester)
Capitol Records TCCL 416 (Cassette)
Released: July 1986
Capitol Records CDCL 416 (CD)
Released: July 1986

World Where You Live (extended version) (Finn)/**Can't Carry On This Way** (Finn)/**That's What I Call Love** (Finn, Hester)
Capitol Records 12 CL 416 (12")
Released: July 1986

Don't Dream It's Over (Finn)/**That's What I Call Love** (Finn, Hester)
Capitol CL 438 (7")
Released: January 1987

Don't Dream It's Over (Finn)/**Don't Dream It's Over** (Finn)/**That's What I Call Love** (Finn, Hester)
Capitol 12CL 438 (12" extended version)
Released: January 1987
Capitol TCCL 438 (Cassette)
Released: January 1987
Capitol 12 CDCL 438 (CD)

Something So Strong (Finn, Froom)/**I Walk Away** (Finn)
Capitol CL 456 (7")
Released: August 1987

Something So Strong (Finn, Froom)/**Something So Strong (live)**
(Finn,Froom)/**I Walk Away** (Finn)/**Don't Dream It's Over (live)** (Finn)
Capitol 12 CL 456 (12")
Released: August 1987

Better Be Home Soon (Finn)/**Kill Eye** (Finn)
Capitol CL 498 (7")
Released: June 1988

Better Be Home Soon (Finn)/**Don't Dream It's Over (live)** (Finn)/**Kill Eye**
(Finn)
Capitol 12 CL 498 (12")
Released: June 1988
Capitol CDCL 498 (CD)
Released: June 1988

Temple Of Low Men
Capitol EST 2064 (LP)/TCEST 2064 (Cassette)/CDP 7487632 (CD)
Released: August 1988
Titles: I Feel Possessed (Finn)/Kill Eye (Finn)/Into Temptation (Finn)/Mansion In
The Slums (Finn)/When You Come (Finn)/Never Be The Same (Finn)/Love This
Life (Finn)/Sister Madly (Finn)/In The Lowlands (Finn)/ Better Be Home Soon
(Finn)

Sister Madly (Finn)/**Mansion In The Slums** (Finn)
Capitol CL 509 (7")
Released: August 1988

Sister Madly (Finn)/**Mansion In The Slums** (Finn)/**Something So Strong** (live)
(Finn)
Capitol 12 CL 509 (12")
Released: August 1988
Capitol CDCL 509 (CD)
Released: August 1988

Chocolate Cake (Finn, Finn)/**As Sure As I Am** (Finn)
Capitol CL 618 (7")
Released: June 1991
Capitol TCCL 618 (Cassette)
Released: June 1991

Chocolate Cake (Finn, Finn)/**As Sure As I Am** (Finn)/**Anyone Can Tell** (Finn)
Capitol 12 CL 618 (12")
Released: June 1991
Capitol CDCL 618 (CD jewel box)
Released: June 1991

Woodface

Capitol EST 2144 (LP)/TCEST 2144 (Cassette)/CDP 7935592 (CD)
Released: June 1991
Titles: Chocolate Cake (Finn, Finn)/It's Only Natural (Finn, Finn)/Fall At Your Feet (Finn)/Tall Trees (Finn, Finn)/Weather With You (Finn, Finn)/ Whispers And Moans (Finn)/Four Seasons In One Day (Finn, Finn)/There Goes God (Finn, Finn)/Fame Is (Finn)/All I Ask (Finn, Finn)/As Sure As I Am (Finn)/Italian Plastic (Hester)/She Goes On (Finn)/How Will You Go (Finn, Finn)

Fall At Your Feet (Finn)/**Don't Dream It's Over** (Finn)
Capitol CL 626 (7" flatpack)
Released: October 1991
Capitol TCCL 626 (Cassette flatpack)
Released: October 1991

Fall At Your Feet (Finn)/**Six Months In A Leaky Boat** (live) (Finn, Finn, Griggs, Rayner, Crombie)/**Now We're Getting Somewhere** (live) (Finn)/**Something So Strong** (Finn, Froom)
Capitol CDCLX 626 (CD flatpack)
Released: October 1991

Fall At Your Feet (Finn)/**Don't Dream It's Over** (Finn)/**Sister Madly** (Finn)/**Better Be Home Soon** (Finn)
Capitol CDCL 626 (CD flatpack)
Released: October 1991

Weather With You (Finn, Finn)/**Into Temptation** (Finn)
Capitol CL 643 (7" single edit)
Released: February 1992
Capitol TCCL 643 (Cassette single edit)
Released: February 1992

Weather With You (Finn, Finn)/**Mr. Tambourine Man** (live) (Dylan)/**Eight Miles High** (live) (Clark, MC, Crosby)/**So You Want To Be A Rock 'n' Roll Star** (live) (MC, Hullman)
Capitol CDCL 643 (CD flatpack single edit)
Released: February 1992

Weather With You (Finn, Finn)/**Fall At Your Feet** (live) (Finn)/**When You Come** (live) (Finn)/**Walking On The Spot** (live) (Finn)
Capitol CDCLS 643 (CD flatpack radio edit)
Released: February 1992

Four Seasons In One Day (Finn, Finn)/**There Goes God** (Finn, Finn)
Capitol CL 655 (7")
Released: June 1992
Capitol TCCL 655 (Cassette)

Four Seasons In One Day (Finn, Finn)/**Dr. Livingstone** (Finn)/**Recurring Dream** (1989 version) (Finn, Seymour, Hester, Hooper)/**Anyone Can Tell** (Finn)
Capitol CDCLS 655 (CD flatpack)
Released: June 1992

Four Seasons In One Day (Finn, Finn)/**Weather With You** (live) (Finn, Finn)/**Italian Plastic** (live) (Hester)/**Message To My Girl** (live) (Finn)
Capitol CDCL 655 (CD)
Released: June 1992

It's Only Natural (Finn, Finn)
Capitol CDCLDJ 661 (Promotional CD)
Released: September 1992

It's Only Natural (Finn, Finn)/**Chocolate Cake** (Finn, Finn)
Capitol CL 661 (7")
Released: September 1992
Capitol TCCL 661 (Cassette)
Released: September 1992

It's Only Natural (Finn, Finn)/**It's Only Natural** (live) (Finn, Finn)/**Hole In The River** (live) (Finn, Rayner)
Capitol CDCLS 661 (CD flatpack)
Released: September 1992

It's Only Natural (Finn, Finn)/**Sister Madly** (live) (Finn)/**There Goes God** (live) (Finn, Finn)/**Chocolate Cake** (live) (Finn, Finn)
Capitol CDCL 661 (CD flatpack)
Released: September 1992

Distant Sun (Finn)/**This Is Massive** (live) (Finn)/**When You Come** (live) (Finn)
Capitol CDCLS 697 (Double digipak with space for second CD of set)
Released: September 1993

Distant Sun (Finn)/**Walking On The Spot** (Finn)/**Throw Your Arms Around Me** (live) (Miles, Archer, Seymour, Waters)/**One Step Ahead** (live) (Finn)
Capitol CDCL 697 (Thinline jewel box; CD fits in double digipak of first CD in set)
Released: September 1993

Alone 1 An Introduction To Together Alone
Promotional-only sampler of Together Alone
Released: September 1993
Titles: Private Universe (Finn)/Distant Sun (Finn)/Nails In My Feet (Finn)/Together Alone (Finn, Hart, Wehi)

Together Alone
Capitol EST 2215 (LP)/TCESTU 2215 (Cassette)/CDESTU 8270482 (CD)
Released: October 1993
Titles: Kare Kare (Finn, Hart, Seymour, Hester), In My Command (Finn), Nails In My Feet (Finn), Black & White Boy (Finn), Fingers Of Love (Finn), Pineapple Head (Finn), Locked Out (Finn), Private Universe (Finn), Walking On The Spot (Finn), Distant Sun (Finn), Catherine Wheels (Finn, Finn, Seymour), Skin Feeling (Hester), Together Alone (Finn, Hart, Wehi)

Nails In My Feet (Finn)/**You Can Touch** (Finn)/**Zen Roxy (instrumental)** (Finn)
Capitol CDCLS 701 (Double digipak with space for second CD of set)
Released: November 1993

Nails In My Feet (Finn)/**I Am In Love** (Finn)/**Four Seasons In One Day** (live) (Finn, Finn)
Capitol CDCL 701 (Thinline jewel box; CD fits in digipak of first CD of set)
Released: November 1993

Nails In My Feet (Finn)/**Don't Dream It's Over** (live) (Finn)
Capitol CL 701 (7")
Released: November 1993

Full House
Capitol CDCHDJ1 (Promotional CD only; only 600 pressed)
Released: 1994
Titles: Don't Dream It's Over (Finn)/Mean To Me (Finn)/Hole In The River (Finn, Rayner)/World Where You Live (Finn)/Sister Madly (Finn)/Into Temptation (Finn)/When You Come (Finn)/Better Be Home Soon (Finn)/Weather With You (Finn, Finn)/Four Seasons In One Day (Finn, Finn)/Italian Plastic (Hester)/Fall At Your Feet (Finn)/Distant Sun (Finn)/Locked Out (Finn)/Pineapple Head (Finn)/Private Universe (Finn)

Locked Out (Finn)/**Distant Sun** (live) (Finn)
Capitol CCL 707 (cassette)
Released: February 1994

Locked Out (Finn)/**Distant Sun** (live) (Finn)/**Hole In The River** (live) (Finn, Rayner)/**Sister Madly** (live) (Finn)
Capitol CDCLS 707 (CD)
Released: February 1994

Locked Out (Finn)/**Private Universe** (live) (Finn)/**Fall At Your Feet** (live) (Finn)/**Better Be Home Soon** (live) (Finn)
Capitol CDCL 707 (CD)
Released: February 1994

Locked Out (Finn)/**Distant Sun** (live) (Finn)/**Fall At Your Feet** (live) (Finn)/**Private Universe** (live) (Finn)
Capitol 10CL 707 (10")
Released: February 1994

Fingers Of Love (Finn)/**Nails In My Feet** (live) (Finn)
Capitol CCL 715 (cassette)
Released: May 1994

Fingers Of Love (Finn)
Capitol CDCLDJ 715 (promotional CD)
Released: May 1994

Fingers Of Love (Finn)/**Skin Feeling** (Hester)/**Kare Kare** (live) (Finn, Hart, Seymour, Hester)/**In My Command** (live) (Finn)
Capitol CDCLS 715 (Double digipak with space for second CD of series)
Released: May 1994

Fingers Of Love (Finn)/**Catherine Wheels** (Finn, Finn, Seymour)/**Pineapple Head** (live) (Finn)/**Something So Strong** (live) (Finn, Froom)
Capitol CDCL 715 (Thinline jewel box; CD fits in with first CD of series)
Released: May 1994

Fingers Of Love (Finn)/**Fingers Of Love** (live) (Finn)/**Love You 'Til The Day I Die** (live) (Finn)/**Whispers And Moans** (live) (Finn)/**It's Only Natural** (live) (Finn, Finn)
Capitol 10CL 715 (10" with gatefold cover)
Released: May 1994

Pineapple Head (Finn)/**Weather With You** (Finn, Finn)/**Don't Dream It's Over** (Finn)/**Together Alone** (Finn, Hart, Wehi)
Capitol CDCL 723 (CD)
Released: September 1994

Pineapple Head (Finn)/**Weather With You** (Finn, Finn)
Capitol CCL 723 (cassette)
Released: September 1994

Pineapple Head (Finn)/**Weather With You** (Finn, Finn)/**Don't Dream It's Over** (Finn)/**Together Alone** (Finn, Hart, Wehi)
Capitol 10CL 723 (10")
Released: September 1994

Recurring Dream – The Very Best Of Crowded House

Capitol CDEST2283 CD
Released: June 1996
Capitol TCEST 2283 (cassette)
Released: June 1996
Titles: Weather With You (Finn, Finn)/World Where You Live (Finn)/Fall At Your Feet (Finn)/Locked Out (Finn)/Don't Dream It's Over (Finn)/Into Temptation (Finn) /Pineapple Head (Finn)/When You Come (Finn)/Private Universe (Finn)/Not The Girl You Think You Are (Finn)/Instinct (Finn)/I Feel Possessed (Finn)/Four Seasons In One Day (Finn, Finn)/It's Only Natural (Finn, Finn)/ Distant Sun (Finn)/ Something So Strong (Finn, Froom)/Mean To Me (Finn)/Better Be Home Soon (Finn)/Everything Is Good For You (Finn)

Recurring Dream – Crowded House Special Edition Live Version

Capitol CDESTX2283 (CD)
Released: June 1996
Capitol 8522482/92 Promotional CD in a gatefold cardboard sleeve
Released: June 1996
Titles: Weather With You (Finn, Finn)/World Where You Live (Finn)/Fall At Your Feet (Finn)/Locked Out (Finn)/Don't Dream It's Over (Finn)/Into Temptation (Finn) /Pineapple Head (Finn)/When You Come (Finn)/Private Universe (Finn)/Not The Girl You Think You Are (Finn)/Instinct (Finn)/I Feel Possessed (Finn)/Four Seasons In One Day (Finn, Finn)/It's Only Natural (Finn, Finn)/Distant Sun (Finn)/ Something So Strong (Finn, Froom)/Mean To Me (Finn)/Better Be Home Soon (Finn)/Everything Is Good For You (Finn)
Live titles: There Goes God (Finn, Finn)/Newcastle Jam(Finn, Hester, Hart and Seymour)/Love You 'Til The Day I Die (Finn)/Hole In The River (Finn, Rayner)/ Private Universe (Finn)/Pineapple Head (Finn)How Will You Go (Finn, Finn)/Left Hand (Finn)/Whispers And Moans (Finn)/Kill Eye (Finn)/Don't Dream It's Over (Finn)/When You Come (Finn)/Sister Madly (Finn)/In My Command (Finn)

Not The Girl You Think You Are (Part 1) (Finn)/**Distant Sun** (Finn)/**Fall At Your Feet** (Finn)
Capitol CDCLS 776 CD
Released: June 1996

Not The Girl You Think You Are (Part 2) (Finn)/**Private Universe** (Finn)/**Fingers Of Love** (Finn)/**Better Be Home Soon** (Finn)
Capitol CDCL 776 CD
Released: June 1996

Not The Girl You Think You Are (Finn)
Capitol CDCLDJ776 (promotional CD)
Released: June 1996

Not The Girl You Think You Are (Finn)/**Better Be Home Soon** (Finn)
Capitol CL776 (7" white vinyl)
Released: June 1996

Instinct (Finn)/**Recurring Dream** (Hooper/Hester/Finn/Seymour)/**Weather With You** (Finn, Finn)/**Chocolate Cake** (Finn/Finn)
Capitol CDCLS 774 (CD)
Released: June 1996
EMI TCCL774 (Cassette)
Released: June 1996

Don't Dream It's Over (re-issue) (Finn)/**Four Seasons In One Day (live)** (Finn, Finn)/**In My Command (live)** (Finn)/**Pineapple Head (live)** (Finn)
Capitol CDCL 780 (CD)
Released: October 1996

Woodface 1997 Bonus Album
EMI MO33861 (Part of EMI Centenary series)
Released: 1997
Demo titles: Chocolate Cake (Finn, Finn)/It's Only Natural (Finn, Finn)/Weather With You (Finn, Finn)/Four Seasons In One Day (Finn, Finn)/How Will You Go (Finn, Finn)

the LYRICS

1 All I Ask

All I ask is to live each moment
Free from the last
Take the road forgotten
Don't leave me here
Oh please let me stray
Far from familiar things

All I ask is to live each moment
All I ask is to live each moment
Free from the last
Strange roads going nowhere in particular

All I ask is to live each moment
All I ask is to live each moment
Free from the last
Free from the last
All I ask

Words and Music by Neil Finn and Tim Finn

2 As Sure As I Am

Make your decision now
Rely on no help from above
Living is luxury
I want everything you throw out
I'll do anything you want to

Please let me go with you
I'll wear the smile on your face
Big, black and beautiful I want it
Everything you throw out
There must be something you can do without

'Cos I am as sure as I am
I couldn't care less for what might go wrong
And I'm as happy as sin in a fear shaken world

I pity the rhino
Down there it's becoming extinct
Killed for a love potion
Sad thing looking like a dead flower
I want it, everything that you throw out

'Cos I am as sure as I am
I couldn't care less for what might go wrong
And I'm as happy as sin in a fear shaken world

Don't wanna be there
Don't wanna be spared
I'll wear the smile on your face

I am as sure as I am
I couldn't care less for what might go wrong
And I'm as happy as sin in a fear shaken world
World, couldn't care less

Words and Music by Neil Finn

3   Better Be Home Soon _____

Somewhere deep inside something's got a
            hold on you
And it's pushing me aside, see it stretch on forever

And I know I'm right for the first time in my life
That's why I tell you, you'd better be home soon

Stripping back the coats of lies and deception
Back to nothingness like a week in the desert

And I know I'm right for the first time in my life
That's why I tell you, you'd better be home soon

So don't say no, don't say nothing's wrong
'Cause when you get back home, maybe I'll be gone

It would cause me pain if we were to end it
But I could start again, you can depend on it

And I know I'm right for the first time in my life
That's why I tell you, you'd better be home soon
That's why I tell you, you'd better be home soon

Words and Music by Neil Finn

4   Black & White Boy _____

Black and white boy, black and white boy
You're so extreme, you're so confused
Colour me in, whatever mood I'm in
I could be still in touch with you

When you're full of the wonder of Spring
It's all sweetness and light that you bring
And a room full of people will fall
            to your infinite charm
But when darkness should quickly descend
You go quietly my miserable friend
To the depths of despair you will crawl
Black and white boy

Black and white boy, black and white boy
You're so extreme, you're so confused
Colour me in, whatever mood I'm in
I could be still in touch with you

When you shake off the shadows of night
And your eyes are so clear and so bright
You make fools of the liars and creeps
Put a rose in my cheeks
But when demons have climbed on your back
You are vicious and quick to attack
And you put on a wonderful show
Do you really, really think I don't know?

Black and white boy, black and white boy
And you run like a cat to the cream
And you're acting so nice it's obscene
And you put on a wonderful show
Do you really, really think I don't know?
Black and white boy, black and white boy
Black and white boy, black and white boy

Words and Music by Neil Finn

5   Can't Carry On _____

Why do I kid myself
Why do I scream for pleasure
It's four in the morning should know better
But she can weave a spell
Want it to last forever
Making me feel like somebody special

Can't carry on this way (*just go to sleep*)
Before it gets too late (*just go to sleep*)
Doing damage to my brain
Well here we go again

Though I look everywhere
I never seem to find it
Always a shadow around a corner
Drown it in alcohol
Stuck in the elevator
Hard to remember in the morning

Can't carry on this way (*just go to sleep*)
Before it gets too late (*just go to sleep*)
Doing damage to my brain
Well here we go again

Tell you about myself
If you're in the mood to listen
Baby you don't know who you're kissing
This is a lonely world
You are a strange companion
When you get what you wanted
You want to leave

Honestly I want to free myself
From the burden of inaction
Honestly I want to raise myself
To any plane I can imagine

Can't carry on this way (*just go to sleep*)
Before it gets too late (*just go to sleep*)
Doing damage to my brain
Well here we go again

Words and Music by Neil Finn

6   Catherine Wheels _____

No night to stay in
Bad moon is rising again
Dice rolls, you burn
Come down, I fear
As that cold wheel turns
I know what I know
Sad Claude's been sleeping around
To stroke the right nerve
Whose needs do I serve
As Catherine's wheel turns

She was always the first to say gone
She's got her Catherine wheels on
Always the first to say gone

Go kindly with him
To his blind apparition
Whose face creases up with age gone grey
You'll be back here one day

She was always the first to say gone
She's got her Catherine wheels on
Always the first to say gone
She's got her Catherine wheels on, wheels on

Catherine wheels
Catherine wheels
Catherine wheels

She's gone, vanished in the night
Broke off the logic of life
He woke, tore the covers back
Found he was empty inside
So they were told when the moon would rise
The best time to leave with your soul

She's gone up towards the light
Watching her whole life unfold
Bruises come up dark
So strong was his hold on her
Regarded by some as his slave
He spoke in a stranger's tongue
Despair us and drive you away
Bruises come up dark

Words and Music by Neil Finn, Tim Finn and Nick Seymour

7 Chocolate Cake

Not everyone in New York would pay
To see Andrew Lloyd Webber
May his trousers fall down as he bows to
The queen and the crown
I don't know what tune that the orchestra played
But it went by me sickly and sentimental

Can I have another piece of chocolate cake
Tammy Baker's got a lot on her plate
Can I buy another cheap Picasso fake
Andy Warhol must be laughing in his grave

The band of the night takes you
To ethereal heights over dinner
And you wander the streets never reaching
The heights that you seek
And the sugar that dripped from the violin's bow
Made the children go crazy
Put a hole in the tooth of a hag

Can I have another piece of chocolate cake
Tammy Baker must be losing her faith
Can I buy another cheap Picasso fake
Andy Warhol must be laughing in his grave

And dogs are on the road
We're all tempting fate
Cars are shooting by with no number plates
And here comes Mrs Hairy Legs

I saw Elvis Presley walk out of a Seven Eleven
And a woman gave birth to a baby
And then bowled 257
The excess of fat on your American bones
Will cushion the impact as you sink like a stone

Can I have another piece of chocolate cake
Tammy Baker, Tammy Baker
Can I buy another cheap Picasso fake
Cheap Picasso, cheap Picasso fake
Can I have another piece of chocolate cake
Kathy Straker, boy could she lose some weight
Can I buy another slice of real estate
Liberace must be laughing in his grave
Can I have another piece of chocolate cake

Words and Music by Neil Finn and Tim Finn

© 1991 & 1998 Roundhead Music and Rebel Larynx Music, USA
EMI Music Publishing Ltd, London WC2H 0EA

8 Distant Sun

Tell me all the things you would change
I don't pretend to know what you want
When you come around and spin my top
Time and again, time and again
No fire where I lit my spark
I am not afraid of the dark
Where your words devour my heart
And put me to shame, put me to shame

And your seven worlds collide
Whenever I am by your side
And dust from a distant sun
Will shower over everyone

You're still so young to travel so far
Old enough to know who you are
Wise enough to carry the scars
Without any blame, there's no one to blame
It's easy to forget what you learned
Waiting for the thrill to return
Feeling your desire burn
And drawn to the flame

And your seven worlds collide
Whenever I am by your side
Dust from a distant sun
Will shower over everyone
Dust from a distant sun
Will shower over everyone

And I'm lying on the table
Washed out, in the flood
Like a Christian
Fearing vengeance from above
I don't pretend to know what you want
But I offer love

Seven worlds will collide
Whenever I am by your side
Dust from a distant sun
Will shower over everyone

As time slips by and on and on

Words and Music by Neil Finn

© 1993 & 1998 Roundhead Music, USA
EMI Music Publishing Ltd, London WC2H 0EA

9   Don't Dream It's Over _____

There is freedom within, there is freedom without
Try to catch the deluge in a paper cup
There's a battle ahead, many battles are lost
But you'll never see the end of the road
While you're travelling with me

Hey now, hey now
Don't dream it's over
Hey now, hey now
When the world comes in
They come, they come
To build a wall between us
We know they won't win

Now I'm towing my car, there's a hole in the roof
My possessions are causing me suspicion
      but there's no proof
In the paper today tales of war and of waste
But you turn right over to the T.V. page

Hey now, hey now
Don't dream it's over
Hey now, hey now
When the world comes in
They come, they come
To build a wall between us
We know they won't win

Now I'm walking again to the beat of a drum
And I'm counting the steps to the door of your heart
Only the shadows ahead barely clearing the roof
Get to know the feeling of liberation and relief

Hey now, hey now
Don't dream it's over
Hey now, hey now
When the world comes in
They come, they come
To build a wall between us
Don't ever let them win

Words and Music by Neil Finn

10   Everything Is Good For You ____

I see a man with a flag and he leads the procession
And a woman shedding tears for a man locked
      in prison
When the two locked eyes and for a moment
      I was taken
And all paths lead to a single conclusion

Everything is good for you
If it doesn't kill you
Everything is good for you
One man's ending is another one's beginning
Everything is good for you

It's a nightmare jump into a restless ocean
Where the reckless come to state their position
Oh and if you come undone it might just set you free

Everything is good for you
If it doesn't kill you
Everything is good for you
One man's ending is another one's beginning

Bring back your head
Here comes trouble
To turn the angry word
Don't cover it up

Everything is good for you
If it doesn't kill you
Everything is good for you
If it doesn't kill you
Everything is good for you
It's good for you

Words and Music by Neil Finn

11   Fall At Your Feet ━━━━━━━━

I'm really close tonight
And I feel like I'm moving inside her
Lying in the dark
And I think that I'm beginning to know her
Let it go
I'll be there when you call

Whenever I fall at your feet
You let your tears rain down on me
Whenever I touch your slow turning pain

You're hiding from me now
There's something in the way that you're talking
The words don't sound right
But I hear them all moving inside you
Go
I'll be waiting when you call

Whenever I fall at your feet
Won't you let your tears rain down on me
Whenever I touch your slow turning pain

The finger of blame has turned upon itself
And I'm more than willing to offer myself
Do you want my presence or need my help
Who knows where that might lead

I fall
Whenever I fall at your feet
Would you let your tears rain down on me
Whenever I fall
Whenever I fall

Words and Music by Neil Finn

12   Fame Is ━━━━━━━━

Fork lightning in your hall
Break the skin when you break the fall
I'll be the one to fix it up
Love children of the new age
Just a hippy with a weekly wage
There's no rebellion just a chance to be lazy

When fame is in your blood
You follow the science of love
Wave the magic wand
And hang on?

The rest of us are living in a daze
Keep thinkin' 'bout the choice to be made
Here come the handmaidens of end time
Lost treasure from a primitive race
All the lives written on your face
Can't fill the canyons of your mind

When fame is in your blood
You follow the science of love
Wave the magic wand
And hang on?

Now you've changed and jumbled the pieces
You've changed, but you were better off before
You talked to a roomful of strangers
Here comes the handmaidens of end time

When fame is in your blood
You follow the science of love
Wave the magic wand
(and hang on?)
And all of your spells will break
And all of your stars will fall
So look out for number one
Fame is in your blood

Words and Music by Neil Finn

13 Fingers Of Love _____

Can you imagine that
An itch too sensitive to scratch
The light that falls through the cracks
An insect too delicate to catch
I hear the endless murmur
Every blade of grass that shivers in the breeze
And the sound, it comes to carry me
Across the land and over the sea

And I can't look up
Fingers of love move down
And I can't look back
Fingers of love move down

Colour is its own reward
Colour is its own reward
The chiming of a perfect chord
Let's go jumping overboard
Into waves of joy and clarity
Your hands come out to rescue me
And I'm playing in the shallow water
Laughing while the mad dog sleeps

And I can't look up
Fingers of love move down
And I won't be helped
Fingers of love move everywhere

And there is time yet
To fall by the way
From the cradle to the grave
From the palace to the gutter
Beneath the dying rays of the sun
Lie the fingers of love

Into waves of joy and clarity
A fallen angel walked on the sea
And I'm playing in the shallow water
Laughing while the mad dog sleeps

And I can't look up
Fingers of love move down
And I won't be helped
Fingers of love move everywhere

There is time yet
For you to find me
And all at once
Fingers of love move down

Words and Music by Neil Finn

© 1993 & 1998 Roundhead Music, USA
EMI Music Publishing Ltd, London WC2H 0EA

14 Four Seasons In One Day _____

Four seasons in one day
Lying in the depths of your imagination
Worlds above and worlds below
The sun shines on the black clouds
Hanging over the domain
Even when you're feeling warm
The temperature could drop away
Like four seasons in one day

Smiling as the shit comes down
You can tell a man from what he has to say
Everything gets turned around
And I will risk my neck again
You can take me where you will
Up the creek and through the mill
Like all the things you can't explain
Four seasons in one day

Blood dries up:
Like rain, like rain
Fills my cup
Like four seasons in one day

It doesn't pay to make predictions
Sleeping on an unmade bed
Finding out wherever there is comfort
There is pain only one step away
Like four seasons in one day

Blood dries up:
Like rain, like rain
Fills my cup
Like four seasons in one day

Words and Music by Neil Finn and Tim Finn

© 1991 & 1998 Roundhead Music and Rebel Larynx Music, USA
EMI Music Publishing Ltd, London WC2H 0EA

15   Hole In The River _____

There's a hole in the river where my aunty lies
From the land of the living to the air and sky
Left her car by the river left her shoes beside
Through the thorns and the bushes I hope she was...
Dreaming of glory
Miles above the mountains and plains
Free at last
We were touched by a cold wind, my father and I
The sound of desperate breathing
             her fear inside us all
She was coming to see him
But something changed her mind
Drove her down to the river
There is no return

There's a hole in the river where her memory lies
From the land of the living to the air and sky
She was coming to see him
But something changed her mind
Drove her down to the river
There is no return

Words and Music by Neil Finn and Eddie Rayner

16   How Will You Go _____

Escape is on your mind again
Escape to a far away land
At times it seems there is no end
To long hard nights of drinking

How will you go
How will you go
Drive through the wind and the rain
Cover it up
Cover it up
I'll find you a shelter to sleep in

I fell over on the couch again
But you know not all sleep is wasted
Your dreams are alcohol inspired
I can't find a better way to face it

How will you go
How will you go
Drive through the wind and the rain
Cover it up
Cover it up
I'll find you a shelter to sleep in

And you know I'll be fine
Just don't ask me how it's going
Gimme time, gimme time
'Cos I want you to see
'Round the world, 'round the world
Is a tangled up necklace of pearls

How will you go
How will you go
Drive through the wind and the rain
Cover it up
Cover it up
I'll find you a shelter to sleep in

Words and Music by Neil Finn and Tim Finn

17   I Feel Possessed _____

She said 'I could never do that
But I know you can, you are my dream'
We are one person, not two of a kind
And what was mine is now in your possession
I could feel you underneath my skin
As the wind rushed in, sent the kitchen table crashing
She said 'Nobody move or
           I'll bring the house down'

I hardly know which way is up or which way down
People are strange, God only knows
I feel possessed when you come 'round

It was one of those times,
           wished I had a camera on me
Six foot off the ground, well I know how that sounds
Look above you and beyond me too
That kind of view don't need an explanation
I'm not lyin', not askin' for anything
I just want to be there when it happens again

I hardly know which way is up or which way down
People are strange, God only knows
I feel possessed when you come 'round

Whenever you invade my home
Everything I know flies out the window
It's above you and beyond me too
I don't want an explanation but
I'll be there when you bring the house down

I hardly know which way is up or which way down
People are strange, God only knows
I feel possessed when you come 'round
People are strange
I feel possessed when you come 'round
I feel possessed, I feel possessed

Words and Music by Neil Finn

18   I Walk Away _____

You came
Out of this world to me
My life
Parted like the Red Sea
We flowed
Easy between the rocks and stones
Never seemed to stop us
The years
Ended in confusion
Don't ask me I don't know what happened
But I am
A man with a mission
Must be the devil I don't know

It's hard to let go
Of all that we know
As I walk away from you
Hurled from my home
Into the unknown
As I walk away from you

Reveal whatever you desire
To you it may be death defying
Black day
In the coldness of winter
Black words
Slipping off my tongue
I say forget it - it's over
As a dark cloud covered up the sun

You know that it's
Hard to let go
Of all that we know
As I walk away from you
The sun always sets
No room for regrets
As I walk away from you

Give it to me
Give it to me
Your inspiration
Give to receive
Find all we need
As I walk away
I walk away

Just a slave to ambition
Tension your permanent condition
So much you've always wanted
Too much givin' you a sore head

I walk away
I walk away from you
As I walk away from you
As I walk away from you

Words and Music by Neil Finn

19   In My Command _____

We're standing in a deep dark hole
Beneath the sky as black as coal
It's just a fear of losing control
You know so well
Don't miss it when the moment comes
Be submissive just this once
Imagine there is something to be done
Some truth to tell

I would love
To trouble you in your time of need
Lose your way
It's a pleasure when you're in my command

Juggle like a diplomat
Struggle to hold on to your hat
Swinging like an acrobat
But time will tell
The clock is dripping on the wall
Listen to the rise and fall
Close your eyes and hear the call
You know so well

I would love
To trouble you in your time of need
Lose your way
It's a pleasure when you're in my command
Put on your wings
You're responsible for everything

Desolate in anger or safe in isolation
You're about to be the victim of a holy visitation
By the rights I have been given

Put on your wings
You're not responsible for anything
I would love
To trouble you in your time of need
Lose your way
It's a pleasure when you're in my command

When you're in my command

Words and Music by Neil Finn

© 1993 & 1998 Roundhead Music, USA
EMI Music Publishing Ltd, London WC2H 0EA

20   In The Lowlands _____

Oh hell, trouble is coming out here
    in panic and alarm
Black shapes gather in the distance
Looks like it won't take long
The first drops land on the window
The first sign that there's something wrong
Light rain and a head full of thunder
Which way? Which way?
Two days till I get to you
I'll be late if I ever get through
Where I go there'll be no kind welcome
Coming down upon me

Time will keep me warm, feel my face
And now the insects swarm in the lowlands
Fear will take the place of desire
And we will fan the flames from on high
Try for heaven's sake

The sky fell underneath a blanket
The sun sank as the miles went by
Sit back with your head on the pillow
When you remember it makes you cry
Ghost cars on the freeway
Like friends that you thought you had
One by one they are disappearing

Time will keep me warm, feel my face
And now the insects swarm in the lowlands
Fear will take the place of desire
And we will fan the flames from on high
From on high

Words and Music by Neil Finn

© 1987 & 1998 Roundhead Music, USA
EMI Music Publishing Ltd, London WC2H 0EA

21 Instinct

I lit the match, I lit the match
I saw another monster turn to ash
Felt the burden lifting from my back
Do you recognize the nervous twitch
That exposes the weakness of the myth

When your turn comes round
And the light goes on
And you feel your attraction again
And your instinct can't be wrong

Separate the fiction from the fact
I been a little slow to react
But it's nearly time to flick the switch
And I'm hanging by a single stitch
Laughing at the stony face of gloom

When your turn comes round
And the light goes on
And you feel your attraction again
And your instinct can't be wrong

And the fearless come and go
Where the true present lies
They're calling down
They're calling down yeah

Calling
Laughing at the stony face of gloom

When your turn comes round
And the days get long
And you feel your attraction to him
And your instinct can't be wrong

Calling down
Calling down

Words and Music by Neil Finn

© 1996 & 1998 Roundhead Music, USA
EMI Music Publishing Ltd, London WC2H 0EA

22 Italian Plastic

I bring you plates from Rome
You say they look fantastic
I say we're having fun
Nothing like that Italian plastic

I bring you rocks and flowers
You say they look pathetic
You pick me up at night
I don't feel pathetic

When you wake up with me
I'll be your glass of water
When you stick up for me
Then you're my Bella Bambina

I say we're on a trip
Looks like we're on vacation
I say we're having fun
In our little constellation

When you wake up with me
I'll be your glass of water
When you stick up for me
Then I'll be your Bella Bambino

Your man from the moon
I'll be your little boy running
With that egg on his spoon
I'll be your soul survivor
Your worst wicked friend
I'll be your piggy in the middle
Stick with you till the end

When you wake up with me
I'll be your glass of water
When you stick up for me
Then you're my Bella Bambina

Who ya gonna take to the ball tonight?
Who ya gonna take to the dance tonight?

Words and Music by Paul Hester

© 1991 & 1998 Warner Bros Music Australia Pty Ltd, Australia
Warner/Chappell Music Ltd, London W6 8BS

23 Into Temptation _____

You opened up your door
I couldn't believe my luck
You in your new blue dress
Takin' away my breath
The cradle is soft and warm
It couldn't do me no harm
You're showin' me how to give

Into temptation
Knowin' full well the earth will rebel
Into temptation
In a muddle of nervous words
Could never amount to betrayal
The sentence is all my own
And the price is to watch it fail
As I turn to go you looked at me for half a second
With an open invitation for me to go

Into temptation
Knowin' full well the earth will rebel
Into temptation
Safe in the wide open arms of hell

We can go sailing in, climb down
Lose yourself when you linger long
Into temptation, right where you belong

The guilty get no sleep
In the last slow hours of morning
Experience is cheap
I should have listened to the warning
But the cradle is soft and warm

Into temptation
Knowin' full well the earth will rebel
Into your wide open arms
No way to break this spell
Break this spell
Don't tell

Words and Music by Neil Finn

24 It's Only Natural _____

Ice will melt, water will boil
You and I can shake off this mortal coil
It's bigger than us
You don't have to worry about it
Ready or not here comes the drop
You feel lucky when you know where you are
You know it's gonna come true
Here in your arms I remember

It's only natural
That I should want to be there with you
It's only natural
That you should feel the same way too

It's easy when you don't try
Going on first impressions
Man in a cage has made his confession
Now you've seen me at my worst
And it won't be the last time I'm down there
I want you to know I feel completely at ease
Read me like a book that's fallen down
          between your knees
Please let me have my way with you

It's only natural
That I should want to be there with you
It's only natural
That you should feel the same way too

It's circumstantial
It's nothing written in the sky
And we don't even have to try

But we'll be shaking like mud, buildings of glass
Sink into the bay, they'll be under the rocks again
You don't have to say, I know you're afraid

It's only natural
That I should want to be there with you
It's only natural
That you should feel the same way too

It's circumstantial
It's something I was born to
It's only natural
Can I help it if I want to

Words and Music by Neil Finn and Tim Finn

25   Kare Kare

I was standing on a wave
Then I made the drop
I was lying in a cave
In the solid rock
I was feeling pretty brave
Till the lights went off

Sleep by no means comes too soon
In a valley lit by the moon

We left a little dust
On his Persian rug
We gathered up our clothes
Got the washing done
In a long-forgotten place
Who'll be the first to run?

Sleep by no means comes too soon
In a valley lit by the moon

I was floating on a wave
Then I made the drop
I was climbing up the walls
Waiting for the band to stop
You can say the magic words
I got my sensors on
And this is the only place
That I always run from

Sleep by no means comes too soon
In a valley lit by the moon

Words and Music by Neil Finn, Mark Hart, Nick Seymour
and Paul Hester

26   Kill Eye

Kill eye, tumbling come out of the sky
Kill eye, a fiery retreat from the stars
Kill eye, came clambering over the wall
Kill eye, halfway to hell and beyond

I wanna be forgiven, I wanna laugh with children
Won't you ever forgive me?
Please, please forgive me!
I wanna hug my mother and the sky above her
I want the earth to open up and hold me

Kill eye, shoot your way out of the bank
Kill eye, watch the security guard
Kill eye, you separate a man from his life

I wanna be forgiven, I wanna laugh with children
I wanna ride the pony, be your one and only friend
Yes, I will love you till the end

Kill eye, halfway to hell and beyond
I wanna hug my mother and the sky above her
I want the earth to open up, the earth to open up

Words and Music by Neil Finn

27   Locked Out

I've been locked out
I've been locked in
But I always seem to come back again
When you're in that room
What do you do?
I know that I will have you in the end

And the clouds they are crying on you
And the birds are offering up their tunes
In a shack as remote as a mansion
You escape into a place where nothing moves

I've been locked out
And I know we're through
But I can't begin to face up to the truth
I wait so long for the walls to crack
But I know that I will one day have you back

And the hills are as soft as a pillow
And they cast a shadow on my bed
And the view when I look through my window
Is an altarpiece I'm praying to
For the living and the dead

Twin valley shines in the morning sun
I send a message out to my only one

And I've been locked out
And I know we're through
But I can't begin to face up to the truth
I wait so long for the walls to crack
But I know that I will one day have you back

And I work with the bees and the honey
And every night I circle like the moon
And it's an act of simple devotion
But it can take forever
When you've got something to prove

I've been locked out
And I've been locked out

Words and Music by Neil Finn

© 1993 & 1998 Roundhead Music, USA
EMI Music Publishing Ltd, London WC2H 0EA

28   Love This Life

Seal my fate
I get your tongue in the mail
No one is wise
Until they see how it lies

Love this life
Don't wait till the next one comes
Gonna pedal my faith
The wheels are still turning round, turn round

And maybe the day will come
When you'll never have to feel no pain
After all my complaining
Gonna love this life
Gonna love this life
Gonna love this life

Love this life
And so they threw you in jail
Whatever you've done
It was a million to one
And don't you just

And don't you just love this life
When it's holding you down?
Gonna pedal my faith
The wheels are still turning round, turn round

So maybe the day will come
When you'll never have to feel no pain
After all my complaining
Gonna love this life
Gonna love this life
Gonna love this life
Gonna love this life
Gonna love

Here's something that you can do
Even if you think that I hate you
Stop your complaining
Leave me defenseless when you

Love this life
Gonna love this life
Gonna love this life
Though you never know why
When you love this life
Gonna love

Words and Music by Neil Finn

© 1987 & 1998 Roundhead Music, USA
EMI Music Publishing Ltd, London WC2H 0EA

29   Love You 'Til The Day I Die _____

There's closets in my head
          where dirty things are kept
That never see the light of day
I want to drag them out, go for a walk
Just to see the look that's on your face
Sometimes I can't be straight
          but I don't want to hurt you
So forgive me if I tell a lie
Sometimes I come on cold but don't believe it
I will love you till the day I die
I believe in doing things backwards
Take heed, start doing things in reverse

Here comes trouble,
          there's nothing wrong when I relax
I'm talking to myself you're coming with me
Teaching you how to distort the facts
Sometimes I can't be straight I don't want to hurt you
So forgive me if I tell a lie
Sometimes I come on cold but don't believe it
I will love you 'til the day I die
I believe in doing things backwards
Take heed, start doing things in reverse

Frost on the window pane, the sound of pouring rain
All makes me glad of you
Though I am far away I am always with you
Know the answer before you know the question
Pull yourself together, baby, push with all your might
I'm alone, always alone
Though I am far away I am always with you

Words and Music by Neil Finn

30   Mansion In The Slums _____

I'd much rather have a caravan in the hills
Than a mansion in the slums

I'd much rather have a caravan in the hills
Than a mansion in the slums
Well, the taste of success
Only lasts you half an hour or less
But it loves you when it comes
And you laugh at yourself
While you're bleeding to death

I'd much rather have a trampoline in my front room
Than an isolation tank
I wish I was a million miles away
From the manager's door
There is trouble at the bank

You laugh at yourself
As you go deep into debt
And you laugh at yourself
While he's breathin' down your neck

Who can stop me with money in my pocket?
Sometimes I get it free
The best of both worlds
The best of both worlds

I'd much rather have a caravan in the hills
I'd much rather have a mansion in the hills
Than a mansion in the slums
I'd much rather, what I mean is
Would you mind if I had it all?
I'll take it when it comes

And you laugh at yourself
While you're bleeding to death
Where somebody else is always
Breathing down your neck
Laugh at yourself
While he's hanging over your head
While he's breathing down your neck
It'll soon be over, with a mansion, mansion
It'll soon be over

Words and Music by Neil Finn

31 Mean To Me

She came all the way from America
Had a blind date with destiny
And the sound of Te Awamutu
Had a truly sacred ring
Now her parents are divorced
And her friend's committing suicide

I could not escape
A plea from the heart
You know what it means to me
She said don't walk away
I'm down on my knees
So please don't be mean to me

So I talked to you for an hour
In the bar of a small town hotel
You asked me what I was thinking
I was thinking of a padded cell
With a black and white T.V.
To stop us from getting lonely

I could not escape
A plea from the heart
You know what it means to me
She said don't walk away
I'm down on my knees
Please don't be mean to me

No I could not escape
A plea from the heart
Mysterious sympathy
I couldn't wait for a chance
To walk out the door
You know what it means to me

I saw you lying in the arms of a poet
I heard him tell you t...tantalizing lies (about me)
Well whad'd'ya know, whad'd'ya know

I could not escape
You're down on the floor
You know what it means to me
I couldn't wait for a chance
To walk out the door
Mean...
You know what it means
In the arms of a poet
You know what it means

Words and Music by Neil Finn

© 1986 & 1998 Roundhead Music, USA
EMI Music Publishing Ltd, London WC2H 0EA

32 Nails In My Feet

My life is a house
You crawl through the window
Slip across the floor and into the reception room
You enter the place of endless persuasion
Like a knock on the door when there's ten
    or more things to do

Who was that calling?
You, my companion
Run to the water on a burning beach
And it brings me relief

Pass through the walls
To find my intentions
Circle round in a strange hypnotic state
I look into space
There is no connection
A million points of light and a conversation
    I can't face

Cast me off one day
To lose my inhibitions
Sit like a lap-dog on a matron's knee
Wear the nails on your feet

I woke up the house
Stumbled in sideways
The lights went on and everybody screamed surprise
The savage review
It left me gasping
But it warms my heart to see that you can do it too

Total surrender
Your touch is so tender
Your skin is like water on a burning beach
And it brings me relief

In the back row, under the stars
And the ceiling is my floor

Words and Music by Neil Finn

© 1993 & 1998 Roundhead Music, USA
EMI Music Publishing Ltd, London WC2H 0EA

33   Never Be The Same _____

Don't stand around like friends
At a funeral, eyes to the ground
It could've been you
And why do you weep for the passing of ages
You slip with the back of your hand
You're taking it out on the one you love

I couldn't believe it
But we might still survive
And rise up through the maze
If you could change your life
And never be the same

How long must I wait
For you to release me?
I pay for each mistake
While you suffer in silence
I could still have an easy life
But the lie ain't worth the living
Once more will I hear you say that

We might still survive
And rise up through the maze
If you could change your life
And never be the same
Never be the same

Don't stand around like friends
At a funeral, eyes to the ground
Don't suffer in silence
'Cause we might still survive
And rise up through the maze
If you could change your life
And never be the same
And every time I hear you
Never be the same
And every time I mess up
Never be the same
Never be the same

Never be the same
And every time I hear you
And every time I mess up
Never be, never be, never be
Never be the same

Words and Music by Neil Finn

© 1987 & 1998 Roundhead Music, USA
EMI Music Publishing Ltd, London WC2H 0EA

34 Not The Girl You Think You Are __

You're not the girl you think you are
They're not his shoes under your bed
He'll take you places in his car
That you won't forget

Ah and all the people that you know
Will turn their heads as you go by
But you'll be hard to recognize
With the top down and the wind blowing, blowing

He won't deceive you or tell you the truth
Woman he'll be no trouble
He won't write you letters full of excuses
Come on believe you have one in a million

You're not the girl you think you are
There's someone standing in your place
The bathroom mirror makes you look tall
But it's all in your head, in your head

He won't deceive you or tell you the truth
Woman he'll be no trouble
He won't write you letters full of excuses
Come on, believe you have one in a million

He won't deceive you or tell you the truth
Come on, believe you have one
You're not the girl you think you are
Believe you have one
You're not the girl you think you are

Words and Music by Neil Finn

© 1996 & 1998 Roundhead Music, USA
EMI Music Publishing Ltd, London WC2H 0EA

35 Now We're Getting Somewhere

It never used to be that bad
But neither was it great
Somewhere in the middle then
Content and much too safe
Ooh tell me please
Why it takes so long
To realize when there's something wrong

Lay me out with your heart
Now we're gettin' somewhere
Push me back to the start
Now we're getting someplace
Take me out let me breathe
Now we're gettin' somewhere
When I'm with you I don't care
Where it is I'm falling

There's money in the Bible Belt
Hugs for daddy too
Three wishes for eternity
We've got some work to do
Ooh tell me please, tell me what went wrong
'Cos I believe there is something wrong

Well lay me out with your heart
Now we're gettin' somewhere
Push me back to the start
Now we're getting someplace
Take me out let me breathe
Now we're gettin' somewhere
When I'm with you I don't care
Where it is I'm falling

When you took me to your room
I swear I said surrender
When you opened up your mouth
I saw the words fall out
Though nothing much has changed
I swear I will surrender
There is pain in my heart
We can choose what we choose to believe

Words and Music by Neil Finn

36 Pineapple Head

Detective is flat, no longer is always flat out
Got the number of the getaway car
Didn't get very far

As lucid as hell and these images
Moving so fast like a fever
So close to the bone
I don't feel too well

And if you choose to take that path
I will play you like a shark
And I'll clutch at your heart
I'll come flying like a spark to inflame you

Sleeping alone for pleasure
The pineapple head, it spins and it spins
Like a number I hold
Don't remember if she was my friend
It was a long time ago

And if you choose to take that path
I will play you like a shark
And I'll clutch at your heart
I'll come flying like a spark to inflame you

Sleeping alone for pleasure
The pineapple head, it spins and it spins
Like a number I hold
Don't remember if she was my friend
It was a long time ago

And if you choose to take that path
Would you come to make me pay?
I will play you like a shark
And I'll clutch at your heart
I'll come flying like a spark to inflame you
I will clutch at your heart
And come flying like a spark to inflame you

Words and Music by Neil Finn

37 Private Universe

No time, no place to talk about the weather
The promise of love is hard to ignore
You said the chance wasn't getting any better
Labour of love is ours to endure

Highest branch on the apple tree
Was my favourite place to be
I could hear them breaking free
But they could not see me

I will run for shelter
Endless summer lift the curse
It feels like nothing matters
In our private universe

I have all I want, is that simple enough?
A whole lot more I'm thinking of
Every night about six o'clock
The birds come back to the palm to talk
They talk to me, birds talk to me
If I go down on my knees

I will run for shelter
Endless summer lift the curse
It feels like nothing matters
In our private universe
Feels like nothing matters
In our private universe

And it's a pleasure that I have known
And it's a treasure that I have gained
And it's a pleasure that I have known
It's a tight squeeze but I won't let go
Time is on the table and the dinner's cold

I will run for shelter
Endless summer lift the curse
It feels like nothing matters
In our private universe

Words and Music by Neil Finn

38 Recurring Dream

Within myself there are a million things
Spilling over, pouring out into a silent stream
Feel the warm wind touch me
Hear the waters crashing
See my windows wiping clean

It's my recurring dream

Within myself a secret world returns
Over and over
Where the white flame of desire burns
Feel the warm wind touch me
Hear the waters crashing
See my windows wiping clean

It's my recurring dream

Within myself there are a million things
Feel the warm wind touch me
Hear the waters crashing
See my windows wiping clean

It's my recurring dream

Words by Neil Finn
Music by Neil Finn, Nick Seymour, Paul Hester and Craig Hooper

39　She Goes On

Pretty soon you'll be able to remember her
Lying in the garden singing
Right where she'll always be
The door is always open
This is the place that I loved her
And these are the friends that she had
Long may the mountain ring
To the sound of her laughter
And she goes on and on

In her soft wind I will whisper
In her warm sun I will glisten
Till we see her once again
In a world without end

We owe it all to Frank Sinatra
The song was playing
As she walked into the room
After the long weekend
They were a lifetime together

Appearing in the eyes of children
In the clear blue mountain view
The colouring in the sky
And painting ladders to heaven
And she goes on and on

In her soft wind I will whisper
In her warm sun I will glisten
Till we see her once again
In a world without end

In her soft wind I will whisper
In her warm sun I will glisten
And I always will remember
In a world without end

Words and Music by Neil Finn

© 1991 & 1998 Roundhead Music, USA
EMI Music Publishing Ltd, London WC2H 0EA

40　Sister Madly

Now you're headin' down to get someone
Should've done what he had to do years ago
The position is comin' through
All the people that you're standing on
All the people that you're standing on
Now you're headin' down to be someone
Someone that you've seen in a magazine
Your premonition is comin' true
Oh baby, you're not so green
Oh baby, you're not so green
Oh baby, you're nutso

Sister Madly, wakin' up the dead
Systematically steppin' on my head
You're Sister Madly, wakin' up the dead
Systematically steppin' on my head

Now you're headin' down to find something
Something you buried in your backyard
The position is comin' through
From all the dirt that you're diggin' up
From all the dirt that you're diggin' up
Now you're headin' down to be somewhere
Somewhere you imagined in your wildest dream
The opposition is comin' through
From all the people that you're standing on
From all the people that you're standing on
And now you'd better take a firm hand

Sister Madly, wakin' up the dead
Systematically steppin' on my head
You're Sister Madly, wakin' up the dead
Systematically steppin' on my head

Now you're headin' down to get someone
Someone that you should've had years ago
The position is comin' through
All the people that you're standing on
All the people that you're standing on
All the people that you're standing on
You're hard to get a hand on

Sister Madly, wakin' up the dead
Systematically steppin' on my head
You're Sister Madly, wakin' up the dead
Systematically steppin' on my head

Words and Music by Neil Finn

© 1987 & 1998 Roundhead Music, USA
EMI Music Publishing Ltd, London WC2H 0EA

41 Skin Feeling

I like the smell of that shop
I like the way it serves me
I like the pigment in your skin
I like the way it moves me
I like kids when they're asleep
Their little arms around you
I like the way you play games
Don't lose that skin feeling

I'm looking old, I'm feeling young
It's the truth my child
My second life has just begun
With this hungry girl

I like black and I like red
I like that orange circle
I like the things that you said
When you were misbehaving
I like people on T.V.
But no one looks like me
I love you, you love me
Don't lose that skin feeling

I'm looking old, I'm feeling young
It's the truth my child
My second life has just begun
With this hungry girl

I love the pigment in your skin
I love the way it moves me
I like the smell of that shop
I like the way it serves me
I like the things that you said
When you were misbehaving
I love you and you love me
Don't lose that skin feeling

I'm looking old, I'm feeling young
It's the truth my child
My second life has just begun
With this hungry girl

It's the truth my child
Let me hold your hand

Words and Music by Paul Hester

© 1991 & 1998 Warner Bros Music Australia Pty Ltd, Australia
Warner/Chappell Music Ltd, London W6 8BS

42 Something So Strong

Love can make you weep
Can make you run for cover
Roots that spread so deep
Bring life to frozen ground

Something so strong
Could carry us away
Something so strong
Could carry us today

Turning in my sleep
Love can leave you cold
The taste of jealousy
Is like a lust for gold

Something so strong
Could carry us away
Something so strong
Could carry us today

I've been feeling so much older
Frame me and hang me on the wall
I've seen you fall into the same trap
This thing is happening to us all

Something so strong
Could carry us away
Something so strong
Could carry us today

Something so strong

Words and Music by Neil Finn and Mitchell Froom

© 1986 & 1998 Roundhead Music and Wyoming Flesh Music, USA
EMI Music Publishing Ltd, London WC2H 0EA
and Warner/Chappell Music Ltd, London W6 8BS

43 Tall Trees

Watch out big ships are waiting
Salt frozen on your cheek
I saw a girl and boy arriving
And a steamer put out to sea

Tall tree stand in the distance
Remember when you were green
Don't wipe the salt from your skin
You must keep running the distance

Sun sleeps on misty morning
Light years from channel 3
I feel halfway to zero
Call me a hero, I might just agree

Tall tree stand in the distance
Remember when you were green
Don't wipe the salt from your skin
You must keep running the distance

And the roses you grow
Have a powerful scent
They'll be breaking your heart
By the morning

I feel halfway to zero
Call me a hero, I might just agree

Tall tree stand in the distance
Remember when you were green
Don't wipe the salt from your skin
Tall tree, tall tree
Don't wipe the salt from your skin
You must keep running the distance
Tall tree

Words and Music by Neil Finn and Tim Finn

44 That's What I Call Love

You take away my air
You make my lungs collapse
I die tonight

Feeling devastated
That's what I call
Livin' in your memory
That's what I call
Tired and deflated
That's what I call
Love

I tidy up your room
You tidy up my life
Show me the door
I'm abandoned here
I'm warm to the core
I can feel
You swim I sink
We never got in that deep
You bend I break
I die tonight

Feeling devastated
That's what I call
Hangin' on and falling over
That's what I call
Tired and deflated
That's what I call
Love

I got a little room
The air's still pretty bad
I die tonight

Feeling devastated
That's what I call
Hangin' on and falling over
That's what I call
Tired and deflated
That's what I call
Feeling devastated
That's
Livin' with a vacuum cleaner
What
Sweepin' up your memory
I call Love

Words and Music by Neil Finn and Paul Hester

45   There Goes God _____

What'll I tell him
When he comes to me for absolution
Wouldn't you know it
Hope I don't make a bad decision

'Cos I'd like to believe
That there is a god
Why sinful angels suffer for love
I'd like to believe
In the terrible truth, in the beautiful lie
Like to know you
But in this town I can't get arrested
If you know me
Why don't you tell me what I'm thinking

Hey don't look now
But there goes God
In his sexy pants and his sausage dog
And he can't stand Beelzebub
'Cos he looks so good in black, in black

Hey don't look now
But there goes God
In his sexy pants and his sausage dog
And he can't stand Beelzebub
'Cos he looks so good in black, in black

Words and Music by Neil Finn and Tim Finn

46   Together Alone _____

Together alone
Above and beneath
We were as close
As anyone can be
Now you are gone
Far away from me
As is once
Will always be
Together alone

Maori Chant

Anei ra maua
E piri tahi nei
E noha tahi nei
Ko maua anake
Kei runga a Rangi
Ko papa kei raro
E mau tonu nei
Kia mau tonu ra

Together alone
Shallow and deep
Holding our breath
Paying death no heed
I'm still your friend
When you are in need
As is once
Will always be
Earth and sky
Moon and sea

Maori Chant

Anei ra maua
E piri tahi nei
E noha tahi nei
Ko maua anake
Kei runga a Rangi
Ko papa kei raro
E mau tonu nei
Kia mau tonu ra
E mau tonu nei
Kia mau tonu ra

Translation:

*Here we are together
In a very close embrace
Being together
Just us alone*

*Rangi the sky-father is above
The earth-mother is below
Our love for one another
Is everlasting*

Words and Music by Neil Finn, Mark Hart and B Wehl

47   Tombstone

Look at all the plans I made
Falling down like scraps of paper
I will leave them where they lie to remind me
From the past a rumour comes
Don't let it keep draggin' you down
Throw the memory in an open fire
You'll be free

Roll back the tombstone
Let the saints appear
Roll back the tombstone
Make a new man out of me

Beware the passenger
The train already left the station
We are neither at home nor at work
We are moving
Listen to the howling of steel
A face betraying no emotion
Like you never had a chance to be
Wild and free

Roll back the tombstone
Let the saints appear
Roll back the tombstone
Till the Lone Ranger rides again
Rides again in your mind
Rode across the open plain
All the way and back again

Words and Music by Neil Finn

48   Walking On The Spot

At odd times we slip
Slither down the dark hole
Fingers point from old windows
An eerie shadow falls
Walking on the spot
To show that I'm alive
Moving every bone in my body
From side to side

Will we be in our minds
When the dawn breaks?
Can we look the milkman in the eye?
The world is somehow different
You have all been changed
Before my very eyes

Walk around your home
And pour yourself a drink
Fire one more torpedo baby
Watch the kitchen sink
Lounging on the sofa maybe
See the living room die
Dishes are unwashed and broken
All you do is cry

Will we be in our minds
When the dawn breaks?
Can we look the milkman in the eye?
The world is somehow different
You have all been changed
Before my very eyes

Dishes are unwashed and broken
All you do is cry

Will we be in our minds
When the dawn breaks?
Can we look the milkman in the eye?
The world is somehow different
You have all been changed
Before my very eyes

Words and Music by Neil Finn

49   Weather With You

Walking 'round the room singing Stormy Weather
At 57 Mount Pleasant St.
Well it's the same room but everything's different
You can fight the sleep but not the dream

Things ain't cooking in my kitchen
Strange affliction wash over me
Julius Caesar and the Roman Empire
Couldn't conquer the blue sky

Well, there's a small boat made of china
It's going nowhere on the mantlepiece
Well, do I lie like a loungeroom lizard
Or do I sing like a bird released

Everywhere you go
Always take the weather with you
Everywhere you go
Always take the weather with you

Words and Music by Neil Finn and Tim Finn

© 1991 & 1998 Roundhead Music and Rebel Larynx Music, USA
EMI Music Publishing Ltd, London WC2H 0EA

50   When You Come

When you come across the sea
Me like a beacon guiding you to safety
The sooner the better now
And when you come the hills will breathe
Like a baby pulled up heaving
From the bottom of the ocean
The sooner the better now
And when you come to cover me
With your kisses fresh like a daisy
Chained up in a lion's den
The sooner the better now

I'll know you by the thunderclap
Pouring like a rain of blood to my emotions
And that is why I stumble to my knees
And why underneath the heavens
With the stars burning and exploding
I know why I could never let you down
When you come

When you come like an iceberg
Floating darkness, smashing my hull
Send me to the bottom of the sea
I should know you better now
And when you come, your majesty
To entrap me, prince of light receding
The sooner the better now

And when you come to cover me
With your kisses hard like armour
The sooner the better now

I'll know you by the thunderclap
Pouring like a rain of blood
To my emotions, hey
And that is why I stumble to my knees
And why underneath the heavens
With the stars burning and exploding
I know why I could never let you down

She came out of the water into my horizon
Like a cumulonimbus coming in from a distance
Burning and exploding, burning and exploding
Like a slow volcano, when you come
When you come, cover the ground
Cover the ground with ashes, with ashes
Baby, when you come, when you come

Words and Music by Neil Finn

© 1987 & 1998 Roundhead Music, USA
EMI Music Publishing Ltd, London WC2H 0EA

51 Whispers And Moans _____

Dull, dull grey, the colour of our times
Cool, cool space that I still hope to find
Far beyond the veil
The sound of whispers and moans
Slow time bomb, the clamour of the street
I hear this town it never goes to sleep
And I will catch the taxi driver
Weeping like a wounded beast

Then I wake up in your room
Share one piece of your life
When tomorrow comes
We may not be here at all
Without your whispers and moans
Here you come to carry me home
Love that sound, time erase
Tension wheels, cool heels
Won't ya come on open the bid before too long

Then I wake up in your room
Share one piece of your life
I'd give anything to be a fly upon the wall
And hear your whispers and moans
I like to hear your whispers and moans
Here you come to carry me home

We are the mirrors of each other
In a lifetime of suspicion
Cleansed in a moment, a flash of recognition
You gave your life for it
Worth it's weight in gold and growing empires
Art collectors and Alans sound investments
Will one day be forgotten, one day be forgotten
Yeah!

Words and Music by Neil Finn

© 1991 & 1998 Roundhead Music, USA
EMI Music Publishing Ltd, London WC2H 0EA

52 World Where You Live _____

Here's someone now whose got the muscle
His steady hand could move a mountain
Expert in bed but come on now
There must be something missing
That golden one leads a double life
You'll find out

But, I don't know where you go
Do you climb into space
To the world where you live
The world where you live

So here we lie against each other
These four walls can never hold us
We're looking for wide open spaces
High above the kitchen
And we're strangers here
On our way to some other place

But I don't know where you go
Do you climb into space
To the world where you live
The world where you live

When friends come round
You might remember and be sad
Behind their eyes is unfamiliar
Do you climb into space
To the world where you live
The world where you live...

Words and Music by Neil Finn

© 1986 & 1998 Roundhead Music, USA
EMI Music Publishing Ltd, London WC2H 0EA

the MUSIC

1 All I Ask

Words and Music by Neil Finn and Tim Finn

2 As Sure As I Am

Words and Music by Neil Finn

I pity the rhino
Down there it's becoming extinct
Killed for a love potion
Sad thing looking like a dead flower
I want it, everything that you throw out

'Cos I am as sure as I am
I couldn't care less
For what might go wrong
And I'm as happy as sin
In a fear shaken world

Don't wanna be there
Don't wanna be spared
I'll wear the smile on your face
I am as sure as I am
I couldn't care less
For what might go wrong
And I'm as happy as sin
In a fear shaken world, world
Couldn't care less

3 Better Be Home Soon

Words and Music by Neil Finn

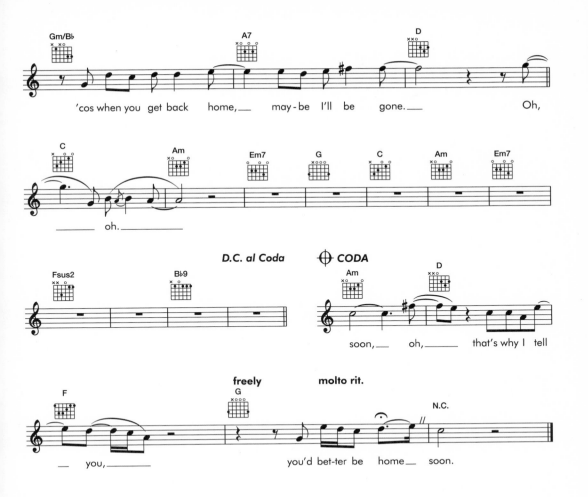

Stripping back the coats of lies and deception
Back to nothingness like a week in the desert
And I know I'm right for the first time in my life
That's why I tell you, you'd better be home soon

So don't say no, don't say nothing's wrong
'Cos when you get back home, maybe I'll be gone

It would cause me pain if we were to end it
But I could start again, you can depend on it
And I know I'm right for the first time in my life
That's why I tell you, you'd better be home soon
Oh, that's why I tell you, you'd better be home soon

4 Black & White Boy

Words and Music by Neil Finn

Black and white boy, black and white boy
You're so extreme, you're so confused
Colour me in, whatever mood I'm in
I could be still in touch with you

When you shake off the shadows of night
And your eyes are so clear and so bright
You make fools of the liars and creeps
Put a rose in my cheeks
But when demons have climbed on your back
You are vicious and quick to attack
And you put on a wonderful show
Do you really, really think I don't know?

Black and white boy, black and white boy
And you run like a cat to the cream
And you're acting so nice it's obscene
And you put on a wonderful show

Do you really, really think I don't know?
Black and white boy, black and white boy
Black and white boy, black and white boy

5 Can't Carry On

Words and Music by Neil Finn

Though I look everywhere
I never seem to find it
Always a shadow 'round the corner
Drown it in alcohol
Stuck in the elevator
Hard to remember in the morning

Can't carry on this way (just go to sleep)
Before it gets too late (just go to sleep)
Doing damage to my brain (just go to sleep)
Well here we go again

Tell you about myself
If you're in the mood to listen
Baby, you don't know who you're kissing
This is a lonely world
You are a strange companion
When you get what you wanted
You want to leave

Honestly, I want to free myself
From the burden of inaction
Honestly, I want to raise myself
To any plane I can imagine

Can't carry on this way (just go to sleep)
Before it gets too late (just go to sleep)
Doing damage to my brain (just go to sleep)
Well here we go again (just go to sleep)
I want to free myself (just go to sleep)
I want to raise myself

6 Catherine Wheels

Words and Music by Neil Finn, Tim Finn and Nick Seymour

No night to stay in, bad moon is ris-ing a-gain. Dice rolls, you burn, come down, __ I fear __ as that cold __ wheel turns, __ I know what I know. Sad Claude's been sleep-ing a-round to stroke the right nerve. Whose needs __ do I serve __ as Cathe-rine's wheel turns. __ She was al-ways the first to __ say __ gone, she's got her Cathe-rine wheels on, al-ways the first to say gone. Go

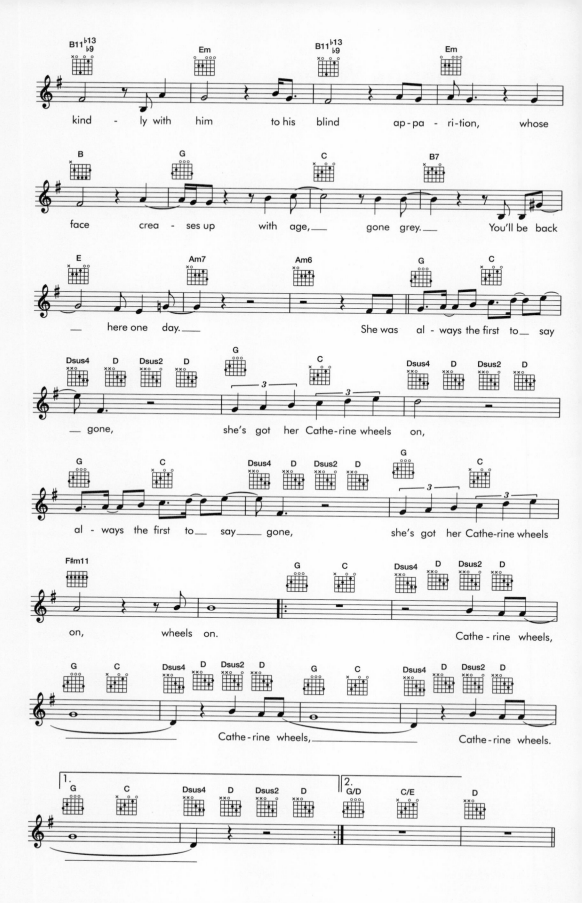

D.%
So strong was his hold on her
Regarded by some as his slave
He spoke as in a stranger's tongue
Despair us and drive you away
Bruises come up dark

7 Chocolate Cake

Words and Music by Neil Finn and Tim Finn

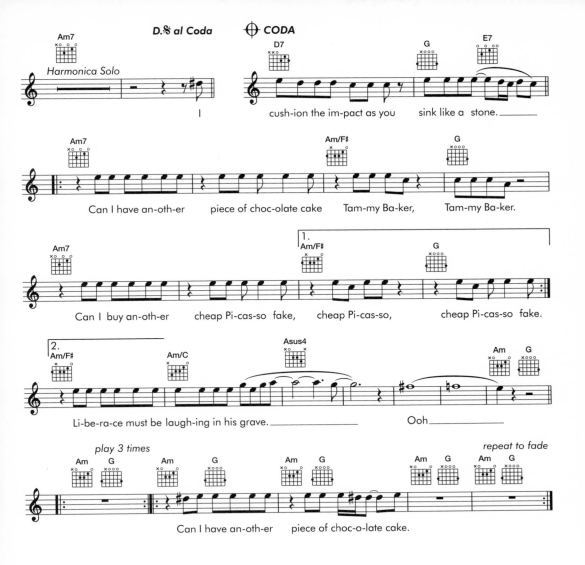

The band of the night takes you
To ethereal heights over dinner
And you wander the streets never reaching
The heights that you seek
And the sugar that dripped from the violin's bow
Made the children go crazy
Put a hole in the tooth of a hag

Can I have another piece of chocolate cake
Tammy Baker must be losing her faith
Can I buy another cheap Picasso fake
Andy Warhol must be laughing in his grave

And dogs are on the road
We're all tempting fate
Cars are shooting by with no number plates
And here comes Mrs Hairy Legs

I saw Elvis Presley walk out of a Seven Eleven
And a woman gave birth to a baby
And then bowled 257
The excess of fat on your American bones
Will cushion the impact as you sink like a stone

Can I have another piece of chocolate cake
Tammy Baker, Tammy Baker
Can I buy another cheap Picasso fake
Cheap Picasso, cheap Picasso fake
Can I have another piece of chocolate cake
Kathy Straker, boy could she lose some weight
Can I buy another slice of real estate
Liberace must be laughing in his grave
Can I have another piece of chocolate cake

8 Distant Sun

Words and Music by Neil Finn

Capo 3

Tell me all the things you would change,

I don't pre-tend to know what you want, when you come a-round and spin my top time and a-gain, time and a-gain.

No fire where I lit my spark,

I am not a-fraid of the dark, where your words de-vour my heart,

1st time
and put me to shame, put me to shame. And your

2nd time
When your se-ven worlds col-lide, when-

-ev-er I am by your side, and dust from a dis-tant sun will

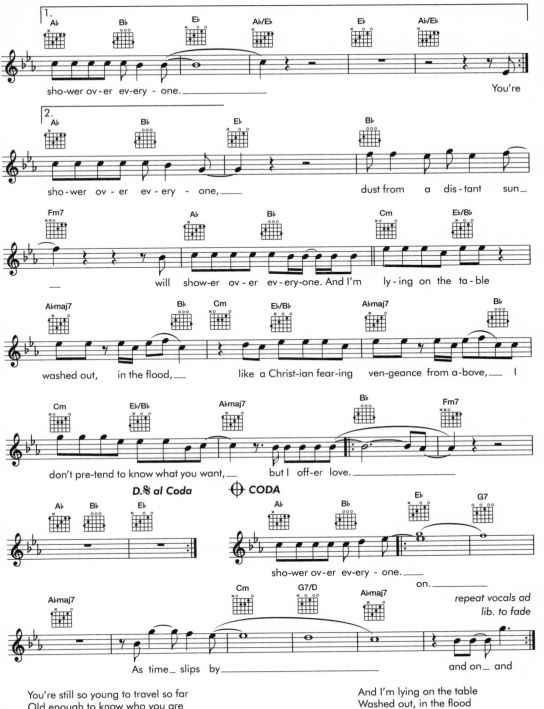

sho-wer ov-er ev-ery-one._____ You're

sho-wer ov-er ev-ery-one,____ dust from a dis-tant sun____

____ will show-er ov-er ev-ery-one. And I'm ly-ing on the ta-ble

washed out, in the flood,___ like a Christ-ian fear-ing ven-geance from a-bove,___ I

don't pre-tend to know what you want,___ but I off-er love._____

D.% al Coda ⊕ **CODA**

sho-wer ov-er ev-ery - one.____

on._____

repeat vocals ad lib. to fade

As time_ slips by_____ and on_ and

You're still so young to travel so far
Old enough to know who you are
Wise enough to carry the scars
Without any blame, there's no one to blame
It's easy to forget what you learned
Waiting for the thrill to return
Feeling your desire burn
And drawn to the flame

And your seven worlds collide
Whenever I am by your side
Dust from a distant sun
Will shower over everyone
Dust from a distant sun
Will shower over everyone

And I'm lying on the table
Washed out, in the flood
Like a Christian
Fearing vengeance from above
I don't pretend to know what you want
But I offer love

Seven worlds will collide
Whenever I am by your side
Dust from a distant sun
Will shower over everyone

As time slips by and on and on

9 Don't Dream It's Over

Words and Music by Neil Finn

Now I'm towing my car, there's a hole in the roof
My possessions are causing me suspicion
    but there's no proof
In the paper today, tales of war and of waste
But you turn right over to the T.V. page

Hey now, hey now
Don't dream it's over
Hey now, hey now
When the world comes in
They come, they come
To build a wall between us
We know they won't win

Now I'm walking again to the beat of a drum
And I'm counting the steps to the door of your heart
Only shadows ahead barely clearing the roof
Get to know the feeling of liberation and relief

Hey now, hey now
Don't dream it's over
Hey now, hey now
When the world comes in
They come, they come
To build a wall between us
We know they won't win
Don't let them win

10 Everything Is Good For You

Words and Music by Neil Finn

11 Fall At Your Feet

Words and Music by Neil Finn

You're hiding from me now
There's something in the way that you're talking
The words don't sound right
But I hear them all moving inside you
Go
I'll be waiting when you call

Whenever I fall at your feet
Won't you let your tears rain down on me
Whenever I touch your slow turning pain

The finger of blame has turned upon itself
And I'm more than willing to offer myself
Do you want my presence or need my help
Who knows where that might lead

I fall
Whenever I fall at your feet
Would you let your tears rain down on me
Whenever I fall, -ever I fall

12 Fame Is

Words and Music by Neil Finn

Fork light-ning in ___ your hall, break the skin when you break the fall, I'll be the one ___ to fix it up. ___

Love child - ren of ___ the new age, just a hip-py with a week-ly wage, there's no re-bel - lion, just a chance to be la - zy. ___ When fame is in your blood ___ you fol-low the sci-ence of love. ___ Wave the ma-gic wand ___ and hang on? ___

hang on?

The rest of us are living in a daze
Keep thinkin' 'bout the choice to be made
Here come the handmaidens of end time
Lost treasure from a primitive race
All the lives written on your face
Can't fill the canyons of your mind

When fame is in your blood
You follow the science of love
Wave the magic wand
And hang on?

Now you've changed and jumbled the pieces
You've changed, but you were better off before
You talked to a roomful of strangers
Here comes the handmaidens of end time

When fame is in your blood
You follow the science of love
Wave the magic wand
(and hang on?)
And all of your spells will break
And all of your stars will fall
So look out for number one
Fame is in your blood

13 Fingers Of Love

Words and Music by Neil Finn

Colour is its own reward
Colour is its own reward
The chiming of a perfect chord
Let's go jumping overboard
Into waves of joy and clarity
Your hands come out to rescue me
And I'm playing in the shallow water
Laughing while the mad dog sleeps

And I can't look up
Fingers of love move down
And I won't be helped
Fingers of love move everywhere

There is time yet
To fall by the way
From the cradle to the grave
From the palace to the gutter
Beneath the dying rays of the sun
Lie the fingers of love

Into waves of joy and clarity
A fallen angel walked on the sea
And I'm playing in the shallow water
Laughing while the mad dog sleeps

And I can't look up
Fingers of love move down
And I won't be helped
Fingers of love move everywhere

And there is time yet
For you to find me
And all at once
Fingers of love move down

14 Four Seasons In One Day

Words and Music by Neil Finn and Tim Finn

Smiling as the shit comes down
You can tell a man from what he has to say
Everything gets turned around
And I will risk my neck again
You can take me where you will
Up the creek and through the mill
Like all the things you can't explain
Four seasons in one day

Chorus:
Blood dries up:
Like rain, like rain
Fills my cup
Like four seasons in one day

It doesn't pay to make predictions
Sleeping on an unmade bed
Finding out wherever there is comfort
There is pain only one step away
Like four seasons in one day

Chorus

15 Hole In The River

Words and Music by Neil Finn and Eddie Rayner

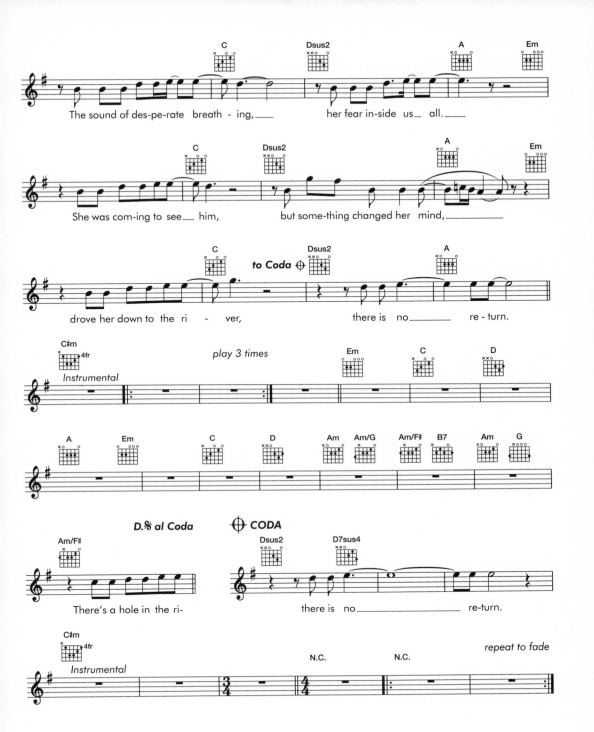

There's a hole in the river where her memory lies
From the land of the living to the air and sky
She was coming to see him
But something changed her mind
Drove her down to the river
There is no return

16 How Will You Go

Words and Music by Neil Finn and Tim Finn

I fell over on the couch again
But you know not all sleep is wasted
Your dreams are alcohol inspired
I can't find a better way to face it

Chorus:
How will you go
How will you go
Drive through the wind and the rain
Cover it up
Cover it up
I'll find you a shelter to sleep in

And you know I'll be fine
Just don't ask me how it's going
Gimme time, gimme time
'Cos I want you to see
'Round the world, 'round the world
Is a tangled up necklace of pearls

Chorus

17 I Feel Possessed

Words and Music by Neil Finn

18 I Walk Away

Words and Music by Neil Finn

♩ = 96

You came out of the world to me, my life___ part-ed like the Red Sea.
We flowed ea-sy be-tween the rocks___ and stones, ne-ver seemed to stop us. The years end-ed in___ con-fu-sion, don't ask___ me, I_____ don't know what hap-pened. But I___ am a man with a mis - sion, must_ be the de - vil, I don't know.___ Fi - nally march - ing to a dif-ferent tune,___ it's hard to let

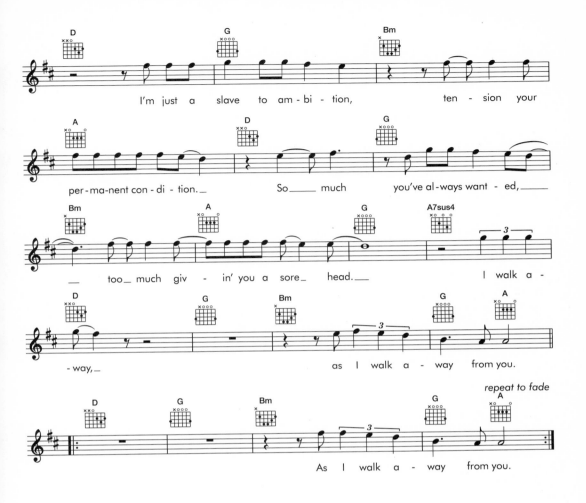

I'm just a slave to am - bi - tion, ten - sion your per - ma - nent con - di - tion.__ So__ much you've al - ways want - ed,____ __ too__ much giv - in' you a sore__ head.__ I walk a - - way, __ as I walk a - way from you.

repeat to fade

As I walk a - way from you.

Reveal whatever you desire
To you it may be death defying
Black day, in the coldness of winter
Black words, slipping off my tongue
I say forget it, it's over
As a dark cloud covered up the sun

You know that
It's hard to let go
Of all that we know
As I walk away from you
The sun always sets
No room for regrets
As I walk away from you

Give it to me
Give it to me
Your inspiration
Give to receive
Find all we need
As I walk away
As I walk away

I'm just a slave to ambition
Tension your permanent condition
So much you've always wanted
Too much givin' you a sore head

I walk away
I walk away from you
As I walk away from you
As I walk away from you

19 In My Command

Words and Music by Neil Finn

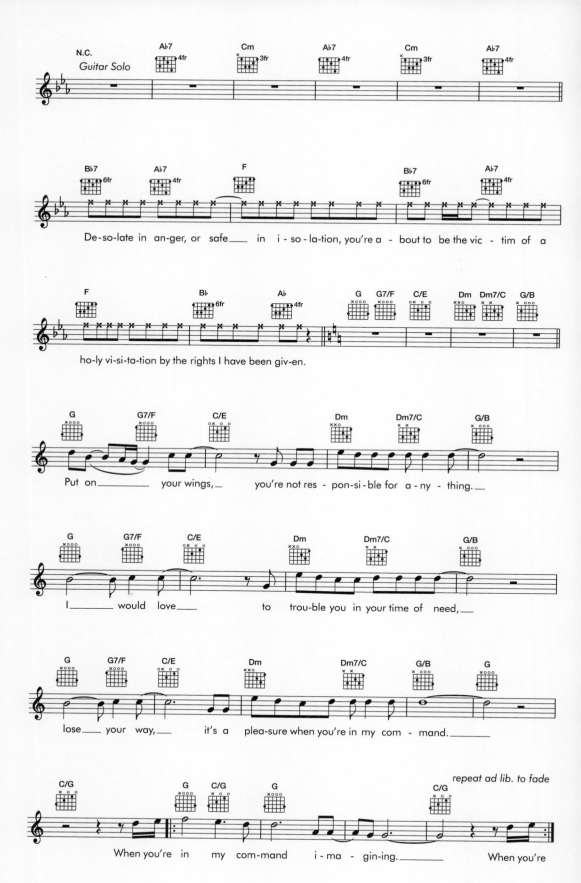

20   In The Lowlands

Words and Music by Neil Finn

The sky fell underneath a blanket
The sun sank as the miles went by
Sit back with your head on the pillow
When you remember it makes you cry
Ghost cars on the freeway
Like friends that you thought you had
One by one they are disappearing

Time will keep me warm, feel my face
And now the insects swarm in the lowlands
Fear will take the place of desire
And we will fan the flames from on high
From on high

21 Instinct

Words and Music by Neil Finn

♩ = 104

I lit the match, I lit the match, I saw an-oth-er mon-ster turn to ash, felt the bur-den lift-ing from my back.__ Do you re-cog-nize the ner-vous twitch that ex-pos - es the weak-ness of the myth.__ When your turn __ comes round__ and the light__ goes on ___ and you feel __ your at-trac - tion a-gain and your in-stinct can't be wrong. Se-par-ate the And the fear-less come and go where the true__ pre-sent lies they're call- -ing down,__ they're call - ing down,_____ yeah.

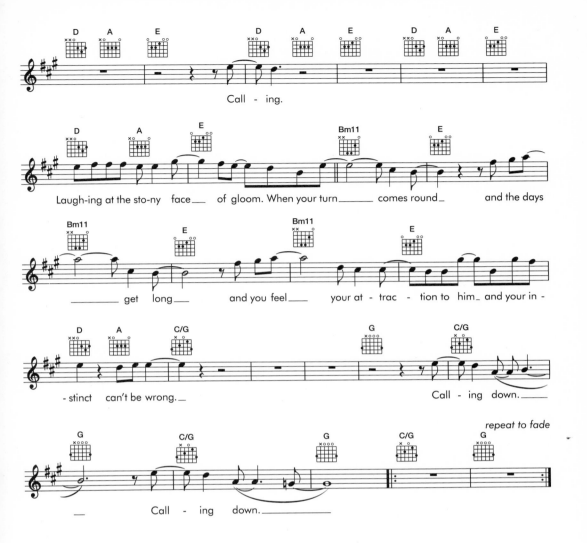

Call - ing.

Laugh-ing at the sto-ny face of gloom. When your turn comes round and the days

get long and you feel your at - trac - tion to him and your in -

- stinct can't be wrong. Call - ing down.

repeat to fade

Call - ing down.

Separate the fiction from the fact
I been a little slow to react
But it's nearly time to flick the switch
And I'm hanging by a single stitch
Laughing at the stony face of gloom

When your turn comes round
And the light goes on
And you feel your attraction again
And your instinct can't be wrong

And the fearless come and go
Where the true present lies
They're calling down
They're calling down yeah

Calling
Laughing at the stony face of gloom

When your turn comes round
And the days get long
And you feel your attraction to him
And your instinct can't be wrong

Calling down
Calling down

22   Italian Plastic

Words and Music by Paul Hester

I bring you rocks and flowers
You say they look pathetic
You pick me up at night
I don't feel pathetic

Chorus:
When you wake up with me
I'll be your glass of water, ah-ha
When you stick up for me
Then you're my Bella Bambina, ah-ha

I say we're on a trip
Looks like we're on vacation
I say we're having fun
In our little constellation

Chorus

Your man from the moon
I'll be your little boy running
With that egg on his spoon
I'll be your soul survivor
Your worst wicked friend
I'll be your piggy in the middle
Stick with you till the end, oh, oh

Chorus

Who ya gonna take to the ball tonight?
Who ya gonna take to the dance tonight?

23 Into Temptation

Words and Music by Neil Finn

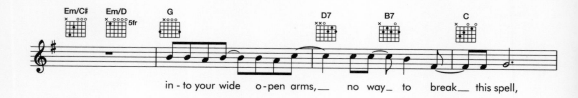

in - to your wide o - pen arms,___ no way___ to break___ this spell,

break this   spell,   don't tell.

repeat to fade

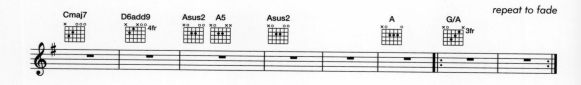

In a muddle of nervous words
Could never amount to betrayal
The sentence is all my own
And the price is to watch it fail
As I turn to go you looked at me for half a second
With an open invitation for me to go

Into temptation
Knowin' full well the earth will rebel
Into temptation
Safe in the wide open arms of hell

We can go sailing in, climb down
Lose yourself when you linger long
Into temptation, right where you belong

The guilty get no sleep
In the last slow hours of morning
Experience is cheap
I should have listened to the warning
But the cradle is soft and warm

Into temptation
Knowin' full well the earth will rebel
Into your wide open arms
No way to break this spell
Break this spell
Don't tell

24   It's Only Natural

Words and Music by Neil Finn and Tim Finn

Ice will melt, wa-ter will boil, you and I can shake off this mor-tal coil, it's big-ger than us, you don't have to wor-ry a-bout it. Rea-dy or not here comes the drop, you feel luck-y when you know where you are, you know it's gon-na come true, here in your arms I re-mem-ber. It's on-ly nat-ural that I should want to be there with you, it's on-ly

It's easy when you don't try
Going on first impressions
Man in a cage has made his confession
Now you've seen me at my worst
And it won't be the last time I'm down there
I want you to know I feel completely at ease
Read me like a book that's fallen down between your knees
Please let me have my way with you

It's only natural
That I should want to be there with you
It's only natural
That you should feel the same way too
It's circumstantial
It's nothing written in the sky
And we don't even have to try

But we'll be shaking like mud
Buildings of glass
Sink into the bay
They'll be under the rocks again
You don't have to say
I know you're afraid

It's only natural
That I should want to be there with you
It's only natural
That you should feel the same way too
It's circumstantial
It's something I was born to
It's only natural
Can I help it if I want to, ooh

25 Kare Kare

Words and Music by Neil Finn, Mark Hart, Nick Seymour and Paul Hester

I was stand-ing on a wave, then I made the drop,

I was ly-ing in a cave in the so - lid rock,

I was feel-ing pret-ty brave till the lights went off.

Sleep by no means comes too soon, in a val-ley lit by the moon.

Yeah.

Slide Guitar Solo

I was float-ing on a wave, then I made the drop,

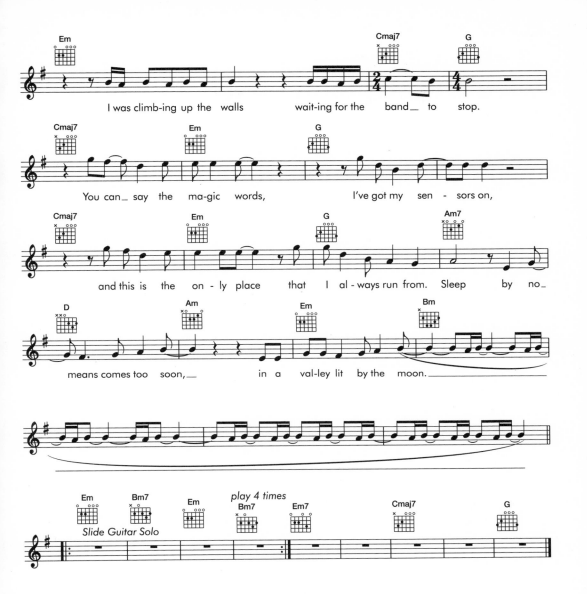

We left a little dust
On his Persian rug
We gathered up our clothes
Got the washing done
In a long-forgotten place
Who'll be the first to run?

Chorus:
Sleep by no means comes too soon
In a valley lit by the moon, yeah

I was floating on a wave
Then I made the drop
I was climbing up the walls
Waiting for the band to stop
You can say the magic words
I got my sensors on
And this is the only place
That I always run from

Chorus

26 Kill Eye

Words and Music by Neil Finn

Tuning for
Guitar boxes

•	B	•	F#	A	C#
•	+2	•	–1	–2	–3

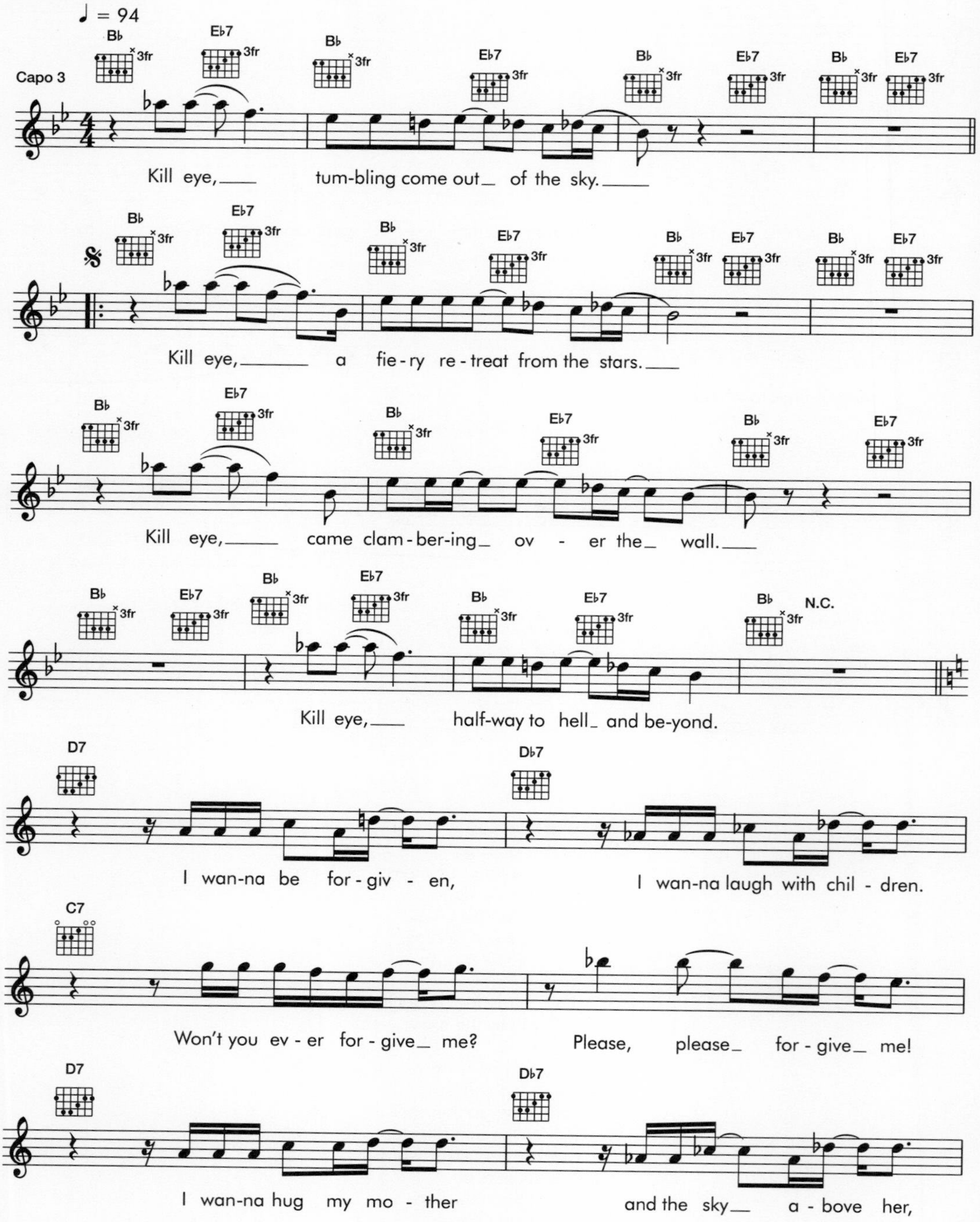

♩ = 94
Capo 3
Bb Eb7 Bb Eb7 Bb Eb7 Bb Eb7
3fr
Kill eye, tum-bling come out of the sky.
Kill eye, a fie-ry re-treat from the stars.
Kill eye, came clam-ber-ing ov - er the wall.
Kill eye, half-way to hell and be-yond.
N.C.
D7 Db7
I wan-na be for-giv - en, I wan-na laugh with chil - dren.
C7
Won't you ev - er for-give me? Please, please for-give me!
I wan-na hug my mo - ther and the sky a-bove her,

Kill eye, shoot your way out of the bank
Kill eye, watch the security guard
Kill eye, you separate a man from his life

I wanna be forgiven, I wanna laugh with children
I wanna ride the pony, be your one and only friend
Yes, I will love you till the end

Kill eye, halfway to hell and beyond
I wanna hug my mother and the sky above her
I want the earth to open up, the earth to open up, ooh

27 Locked Out

Words and Music by Neil Finn

Twin val-ley shines___ in the morn-ing sun.___

I send a mess-age out___ to my on-ly one.___ And I've been locked

CODA

some-thing to prove. I've been locked out, and I've been locked

out, and I've been locked out.___

I've been locked out
And I know we're through
But I can't begin to face up to the truth
I wait so long for the walls to crack
But I know that I will one day have you back

And the hills are as soft as a pillow
And they cast a shadow on my bed
And the view when I look through my window
Is an altarpiece I'm praying to
For the living and the dead

Twin valley shines in the morning sun
I send a message out to my only one

And I've been locked out
And I know we're through
But I can't begin to face up to the truth
And I wait so long for the walls to crack
But I know that I will one day have you back, yes I will

And I work with the bees and the honey
And every night I circle like the moon
And it's an act of simple devotion
But it can take forever
When you've got something to prove

I've been locked out
And I've been locked out

28 Love This Life

Words and Music by Neil Finn

Capo 4

Seal my fate,_ I get your _ tongue in the mail._ No one is wise, un-til they _ see how it lies._ Love this life,_____ don't wait till the _ next one____ comes. Gon-na pe-dal my faith, the wheels are _ still turn-ing round,_ turn round._ And may-be the day_ will come, _ when you'll ne-ver have to feel_ no pain._____ Af-ter all my com-plain-ing, gon-na love this_ life,_ gon-na love this_ life,_ gon-na love this life._ love this life,_ gon-na love this life,_ gon-na love.

Love this life
And so they threw you in jail
Whatever you've done
It was a million to one
And don't you just

And don't you just love this life
When it's holding you down?
Gonna pedal my faith
The wheels are still turning round, turn round

So maybe the day will come
When you'll never have to feel no pain
After all my complaining
Gonna love this life
Gonna love

Here's something that you can do
Even if you think that I hate you
Stop your complaining
Leave me defenseless

When you love this life
Gonna love this life
Though you never know why
When you love this life
Gonna love

29 Love You 'Til The Day I Die

Words and Music by Neil Finn

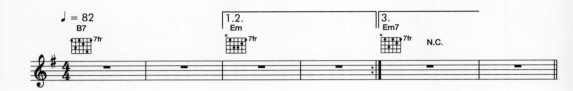

There's clos-ets in___ my head, where dir-ty things are kept, that

ne-ver see___ the light of day._ I want to drag them out,

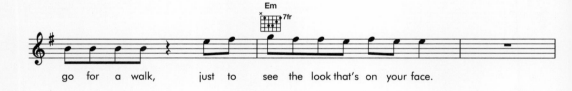

go for a walk, just to see the look that's on your face.

Some-times I can't be straight, I don't want to hurt___ you, so for-

- give me if I tell a lie.___ Some-times I come on cold,

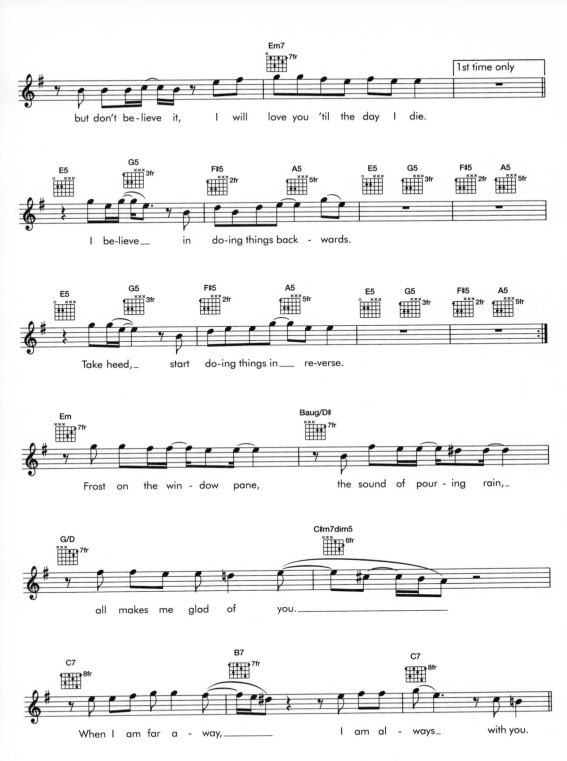

but don't be-lieve it, I will love you 'til the day I die.

I be-lieve__ in do-ing things back - wards.

Take heed,_ start do-ing things in__ re-verse.

Frost on the win - dow pane, the sound of pour - ing rain,_

all makes me glad of you._____

When I am far a - way,_____ I am al - ways_ with you.

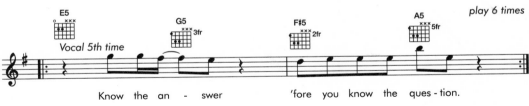

Vocal 5th time

Know the an - swer 'fore you know the ques - tion.

Pull your-self to-ge-ther, ba-by, push with all_ your_ might. I'm_ a-lone,

_____ al - ways a - lone,_____

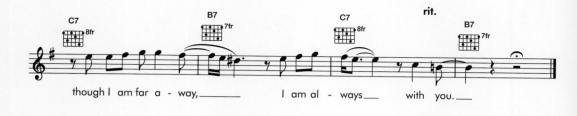

though I am far a - way,_____ I am al - ways_ with you._

Here comes trouble
There's nothing wrong when I relax
I'm talking to myself
You're coming with me
Teaching you how to distort the facts

Sometimes I can't be straight
I don't want to hurt you
So forgive me if I tell a lie
Sometimes I come on cold
But don't believe it
I will love you 'til the day I die

I believe in doing things backwards
Take heed, start doing things in reverse

Frost on the window pane
The sound of pouring rain
All makes me glad of you
When I am far away
I am always with you

Know the answer
Before you know the question
Pull yourself together, baby
Push with all your might
I'm alone, always alone
Though I am far away
I am always with you

30   Mansion In The Slums

Words and Music by Neil Finn

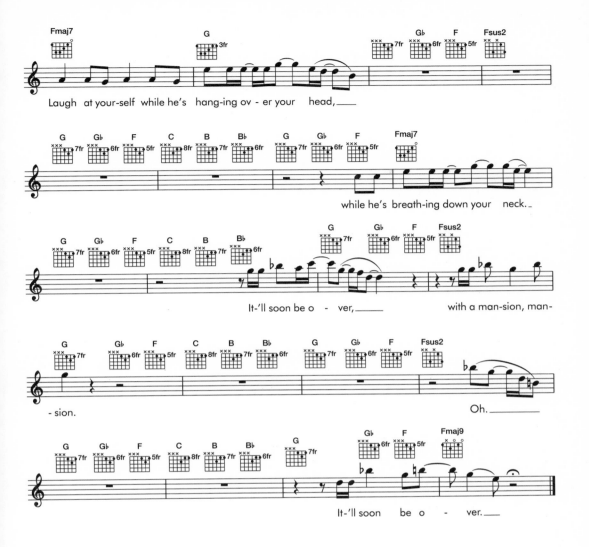

I'd much rather have a trampoline in my front room
Than an isolation tank
I wish I was a million miles away
From the manager's door
There is trouble at the bank

You laugh at yourself
As you go deep into debt
And you laugh at yourself
While he's breathin' down your neck

Who can stop me with money in my pocket?
Sometimes I get it free
The best of both worlds
The best of both worlds

I'd much rather have a caravan in the hills
I'd much rather have a mansion in the hills
Than a mansion in the slums
I'd much rather, what I mean is
Would you mind if I had it all?
I'll take it when it comes

And you laugh at yourself
While you're bleeding to death
When somebody else is always
Breathing down your neck
Laugh at yourself
While he's hanging over your head
While he's breathing down your neck
It'll soon be over, with a mansion, mansion
Oh, it'll soon be over

31 Mean To Me

Words and Music by Neil Finn

walk out the door._____ Mean,_____

I could not es-cape,__ you're down on your knees,_____ you know what it means,

repeat ad lib. to fade

__ what it means.

So I talked to you for an hour
In the bar of a small town hotel
And you asked me what I was thinking
I was thinking of a padded cell
With a black and white T.V.
To stop us from getting lonely

I could not escape
A plea from the heart
You know what it means to me
You said don't walk away
I'm down on my knees
Please don't be mean to me
You know I could not escape
A plea from the heart
Mysterious sympathy
I couldn't wait for a chance
To walk out the door
You know what it means to me, ah

I saw you lying in the arms of a poet
I heard him tell you tantalizing lies
Whad'd'ya know, whad'd'ya know

I could not escape
You're down on the floor
You know what it means to me
I couldn't wait for a chance
Walk out the door
Mean . . .
I could not escape
You're down on your knees
You know what it means
What it means

32 Nails In My Feet

Words and Music by Neil Finn

My life is a house, you crawl through the win-dow, slip a-cross the floor, and in-to the re-cep-tion room. You en-ter the place of end-less per-sua-sion, like a knock on the door when there's ten or more things to do. Who was that call-ing? You, my com-pan-ion run to the wa-ter on a burn-ing beach, and it brings me re-lief. Pass through the knee, wear the nails on your feet.

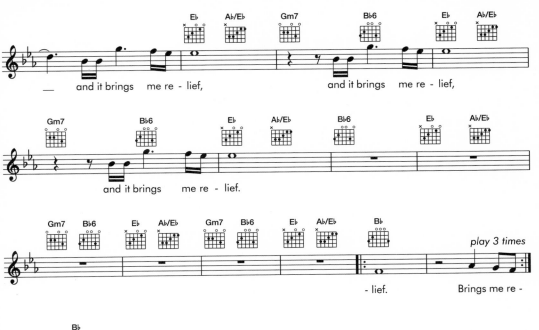

and it brings me re - lief, and it brings me re - lief,

and it brings me re - lief.

play 3 times

- lief. Brings me re -

repeat ad lib. to fade

In the back row___ and un-der the stars,___ and the ceil - ing is my floor.

Pass through the walls
To find my intentions
Circle round in a strange hypnotic state
I look into space
There is no connection
A million points of light
And a conversation I can't face

Cast me off one day
To lose my inhibitions
Sit like a lap-dog on a matron's knee
Wear the nails on your feet

I woke up the house
Stumbled in sideways
The lights went on
And everybody screamed surprise
The savage review
It left me gasping
But it warms my heart
To see that you can do it too

Total surrender
Your touch is so tender
Your skin is like water on a burning beach
And it brings me relief

In the back row, under the stars
And the ceiling is my floor

33 Never Be The Same

Words and Music by Neil Finn

Don't stand a - round ___ like ___ friends at a fu - neral, ___

eyes to the ground, it could-'ve been you. ___ And

why do you weep ___ for the pas - sing of a - ges?

You slip with the back of your hand, you're tak-ing it out ___ on the one ___ you love.

I could-n't be-lieve ___ it, _____ but we might still ___ sur-vive, _____ and

34 Not The Girl You Think You Are

Words and Music by Neil Finn

He won't de-ceive you__ or tell you the truth.__

Come on, be - lieve you have one. You're not the

girl you think you are,__ oh,_____ be -

- lieve you have one. You're not the girl you think you are.

You're not the girl you think you are
There's someone's standing in your place
The bathroom mirror makes you look tall
But it's all in your head, in your head

He won't deceive you or tell you the truth
Woman he'll be no trouble
He won't write you letters full of excuses
Come on, believe you have one in a million

He won't deceive you or tell you the truth
Come on, believe you have one
You're not the girl you think you are
Believe you have one
You're not the girl you think you are

35 Now We're Getting Somewhere

Words and Music by Neil Finn

_____ in my heart, _____ oh, _____ we can choose

_____ what we choose_ to be - lieve. _____

repeat to fade

There's money in the Bible Belt
Hugs for daddy too
Three wishes for eternity
We've got some work to do
Oh, tell me please, why it takes so long
I believe there is something wrong

Well, lay me out with your heart
Now we're gettin' somewhere
Push me back to the start
Now we're gettin' someplace
Take me out, let me breathe
Now we're gettin' somewhere
When I'm with you
I don't care where it is I'm falling

Oh, tell me please, tell me what went wrong
'Cos I believe that there is something wrong

Well, lay me out
Now we're gettin' somewhere
Push me back
Now we're gettin' somewhere
Take me out, let me breathe
Now we're gettin' somewhere
When I'm with you
I don't care where it is I'm falling

When you took me to your room
I, I swear I said surrender
And when you opened up your mouth
I saw the words fall out
And though nothing much has changed
I swear I will surrender
And there is pain in my heart, oh
We can choose what we choose to believe

36   Pineapple Head

Words and Music by Neil Finn

De - tec - tive is flat,   no long - er is al - ways flat out,   got the num - ber of the get - a - way car, did - n't get ve - ry far.   As   And if_____ you choose   to take_____ that path,   I will play you   like a   shark,___   and I'll   clutch   at your   heart,   I'll come fly - ing   like a   spark___   to in - flame   you.

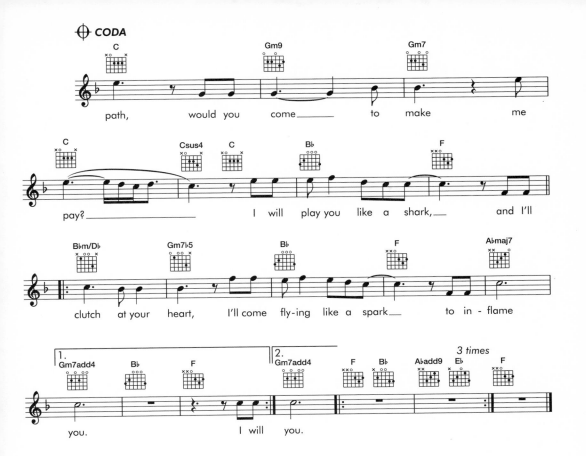

⊕ CODA

path,   would you   come_____   to   make   me

pay?_____   I   will   play you   like a   shark,___   and I'll

clutch   at your   heart,   I'll come   fly-ing   like a   spark___   to in - flame

you.   I will   you.

As lucid as hell and these images
Moving so fast like a fever
So close to the bone
I don't feel too well

And if you choose to take that path
I will play you like a shark
And I'll clutch at your heart
I'll come flying like a spark to inflame you

Sleeping alone for pleasure
The pineapple head, it spins and it spins
Like a number I hold
Don't remember if she was my friend
It was a long time ago

And if you choose to take that path
I will play you like a shark
And I'll clutch at your heart
I'll come flying like a spark to inflame you

Sleeping alone for pleasure
The pineapple head, it spins and it spins
Like a number I hold
Don't remember if she was my friend
It was a long time ago

And if you choose to take that path
Would you come to make me pay?
I will play you like a shark
And I'll clutch at your heart
I'll come flying like a spark to inflame you
I will clutch at your heart
And come flying like a spark to inflame you

37 Private Universe

Words and Music by Neil Finn

No time, no place to talk a-bout the wea-ther, the pro-mise of love is hard __ to ig - nore. You said the chance was-n't get-ting a - ny bet-ter, la-bour of love __ is ours __ to en - dure. High-est branch on the ap - ple tree, __ it was my fav - ourite place __ to be. __ I could hear them break-ing free, but they could not see __ me. __ I will run __ for shel - ter, end-less sum - mer, lift

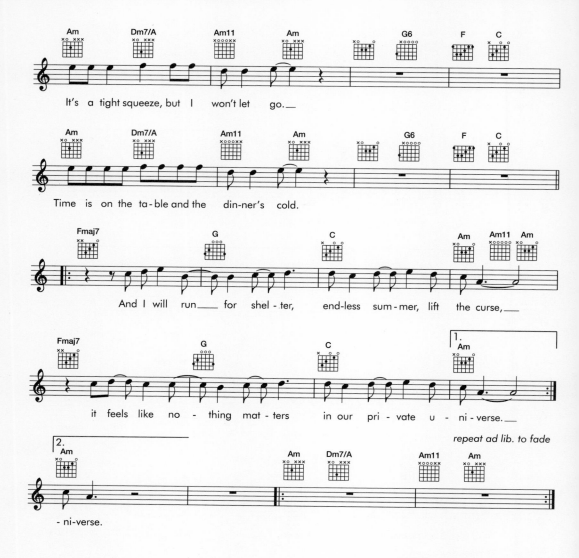

It's a tight squeeze, but I won't let go.—

Time is on the ta - ble and the din - ner's cold.

And I will run___ for shel - ter, end - less sum - mer, lift the curse,___

it feels like no - thing mat - ters in our pri - vate u - ni - verse.—

1.

repeat ad lib. to fade

2.

- ni-verse.

I have all I want, is that simple enough?
A whole lot more I'm thinking of
Every night about six o'clock
The birds come back to the palm to talk
They talk to me, birds talk to me
If I go down on my knees

I will run for shelter
Endless summer lift the curse
It feels like nothing matters
In our private universe
Feels like nothing matters
In our private universe

And it's a pleasure that I have known, ooh
And it's a treasure that I have gained, ooh
And it's a pleasure that I have known, oh

It's a tight squeeze but I won't let go
Time is on the table and the dinner's cold

I will run for shelter
Endless summer lift the curse
It feels like nothing matters
In our private universe

38 Recurring Dream

Words by Neil Finn
Music by Neil Finn, Nick Seymour, Paul Hester and Craig Hooper

39 She Goes On

Words and Music by Neil Finn

Pret-ty soon you'll be a-ble to re-mem-ber her, ly-ing in the gar - den sing-

- ing. Right where she'll al - ways be,_____ the door is____

__ al - ways o - pen. This is the place__ that I__ loved

__ her and these are the friends that she had.___

Long may the moun-tain ring___ to__ the__ sound of her laugh-

- ter and she goes on____ and_ on._____ In her soft__ wind I__ will whis-

She goes on,___ she goes on,_____ she goes on.___

We owe it all to Frank Sinatra
The song was playing
As she walked into the room
After the long weekend
They were a lifetime together
Appearing in the eyes of children
In the clear blue mountain view
The colouring in the sky
And painting ladders to heaven
And she goes on and on

In her soft wind I will whisper
In her warm sun I will glisten
Till we see her once again
In a world without end

In her soft wind I will whisper
In her warm sun I will glisten
And I always will remember
In a world without end

She goes on
She goes on
She goes on

40 Sister Madly

Words and Music by Neil Finn

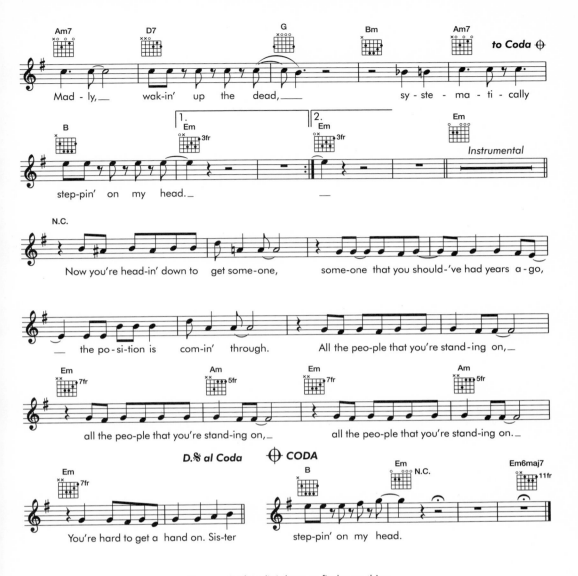

Now you're headin' down to find something
Something you buried in your backyard
The position is comin' through
From all the dirt that you're diggin' up
From all the dirt that you're diggin' up
Now you're headin' down to be somewhere
Somewhere you imagined in your wildest dream
The opposition is comin' through
From all the people that you're standing on
From all the people that you're standing on
And now you'd better take a firm hand

Chorus:
Sister Madly, wakin' up the dead
Systematically steppin' on my head
You're Sister Madly, wakin' up the dead
Systematically steppin' on my head

Now you're heading down to get someone
Someone that you should've had years ago
The position is coming through
All the people that you're standing on
All the people that you're standing on
You're hard to get a hand on

Chorus

41 Skin Feeling

Words and Music by Paul Hester

I like the __ smell of that shop, I like the way it serves me.

I like the pig - ment in your skin, __ I like the way it moves me.

I like kids when they're a - sleep, their lit-tle arms a - round you.

I like the way you play games, don't lose that skin __ feel-ing.

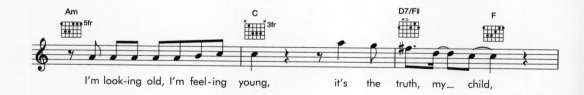

I'm look-ing old, I'm feel-ing young, it's the truth, my __ child,

my se-cond life has just be - gun, with this hun - gry __ girl. __

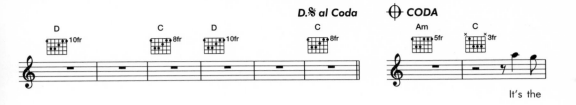

D.%. al Coda   ⊕ CODA

It's the

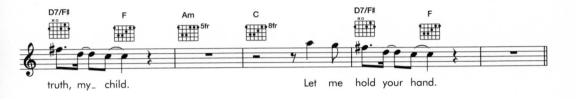

truth, my_ child.   Let me hold your hand.

Rhythm   *ad lib. to fade*

I like black and I like red
I like that orange circle
I like the things that you said
When you were misbehaving
I like people on T.V.
But no one looks like me
I love you, you love me
Don't lose that skin feeling

I'm looking old, I'm feeling young
It's the truth my child
My second life has just begun
With this hungry girl

I love the pigment in your skin
I love the way it moves me
I like the smell of that shop
I like the way it serves me
I like the things that you said
When you were misbehaving
I love you and you love me
Don't lose that skin feeling

I'm looking old, I'm feeling young
It's the truth my child
My second life has just begun
With this hungry girl

It's the truth my child
Let me hold your hand

42 Something So Strong

Words and Music by Neil Finn and Mitchell Froom

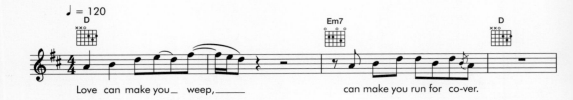

Love can make you weep, can make you run for co-ver.

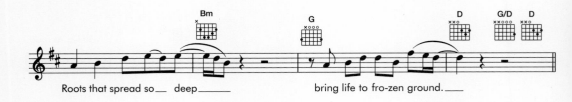

Roots that spread so deep bring life to fro-zen ground.

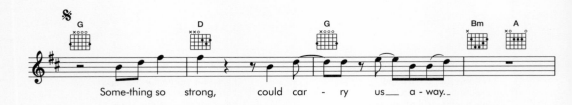

Some-thing so strong, could car - ry us a - way.

Some-thing so strong, could car - ry us to-day.

I've been feel-ing so much old - er, frame me and

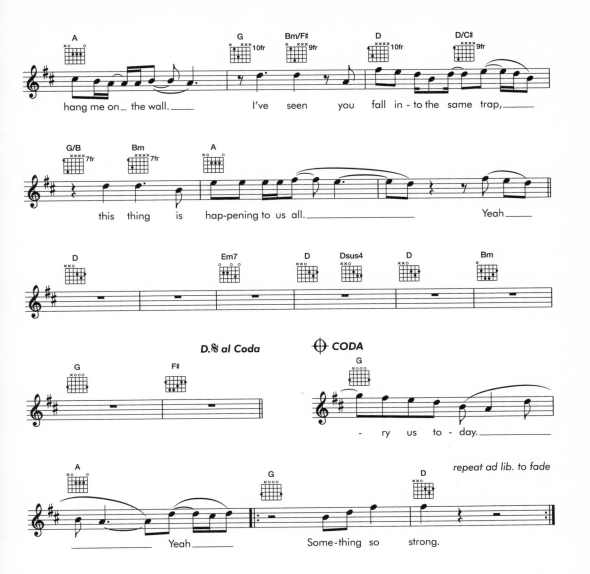

hang me on_ the wall. _____ I've seen you fall in - to the same trap, _____

this thing is hap-pening to us all. _____ Yeah _____

D.%̸ al Coda

$\oplus$ **CODA**

- ry us to - day. _____

repeat ad lib. to fade

_____ Yeah _____ Some-thing so strong.

Turning in my sleep
Love can leave you cold
The taste of jealousy
Is like a lust for gold

Something so strong
Could carry us away
Something so strong
Could carry us today

I've been feeling so much older
Frame me and hang me on the wall
I've seen you fall into the same trap
This thing is happening to us all

Something so strong
Could carry us away
Something so strong
Could carry us today, yeah
Something so strong

43   Tall Trees

Words and Music by Neil Finn and Tim Finn

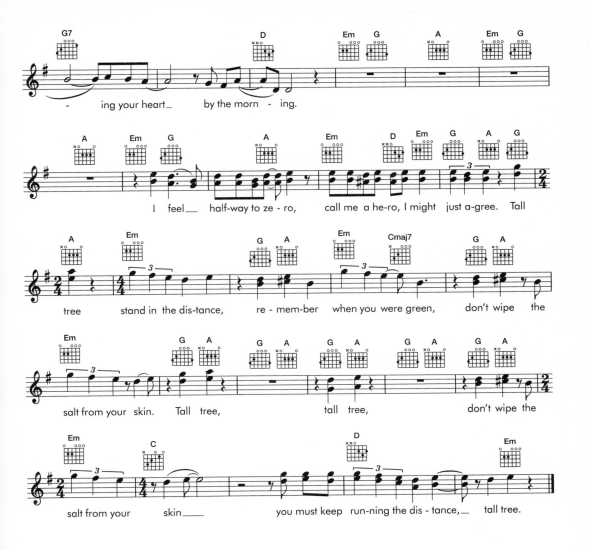

ing your heart__ by the morn - ing.

I feel__ half-way to ze - ro, call me a he-ro, I might just a-gree. Tall

tree stand in the dis-tance, re - mem-ber when you were green, don't wipe the

salt from your skin. Tall tree, tall tree, don't wipe the

salt from your skin___ you must keep run-ning the dis - tance,__ tall tree.

Sun sleeps on misty morning
Light years from channel 3
I feel halfway to zero
Call me a hero, I might just agree

Tall tree stand in the distance
Remember when you were green
Don't wipe the salt from your skin
You must keep running the distance

And the roses you grow
Have a powerful scent
They'll be breaking your heart
By the morning

I feel halfway to zero
Call me a hero, I might just agree

Tall tree stand in the distance
Remember when you were green
Don't wipe the salt from your skin
Tall tree, tall tree
Don't wipe the salt from your skin
You must keep running the distance
Tall tree

44 That's What I Call Love

Words and Music by Neil Finn and Paul Hester

45 There Goes God

Words and Music by Neil Finn and Tim Finn

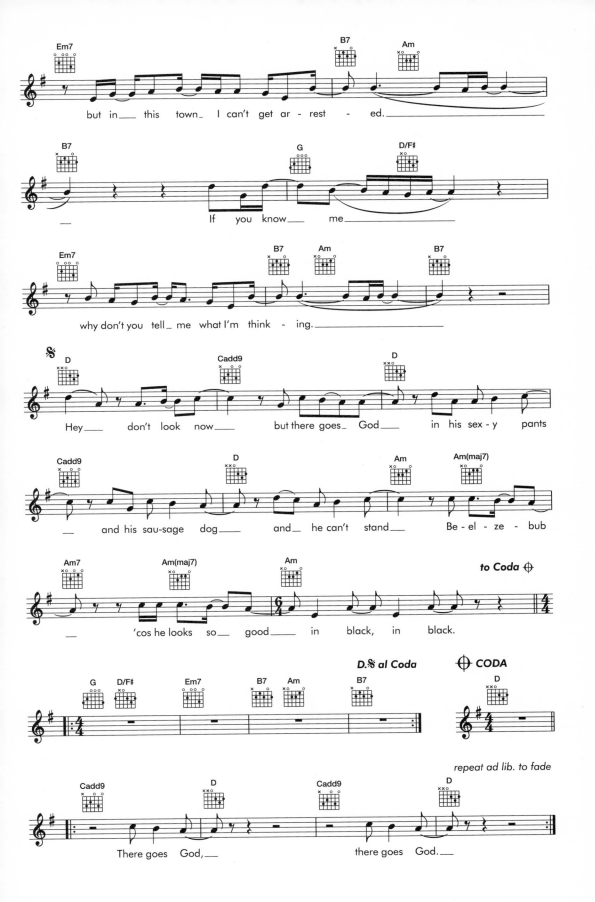

46　Together Alone

Words and Music by Neil Finn, Mark Hart and B Wehl

47 Tombstone

Words and Music by Neil Finn

Look at all the plans__ I made, fall-ing down like scraps of pa - per.

I will leave them where__ they lie__ to re - mind_____ me.

From the past a ru - mour comes, don't let it keep drag-gin' you down.

Throw the mem-ory in an o-pen fire__ and you'll be free._____

Roll back the tomb - stone, let the saints ap - pear._____

Roll back the tomb - stone, and make a new man out_____ of me.

__ a-gain, rides a-gain in your mind._____

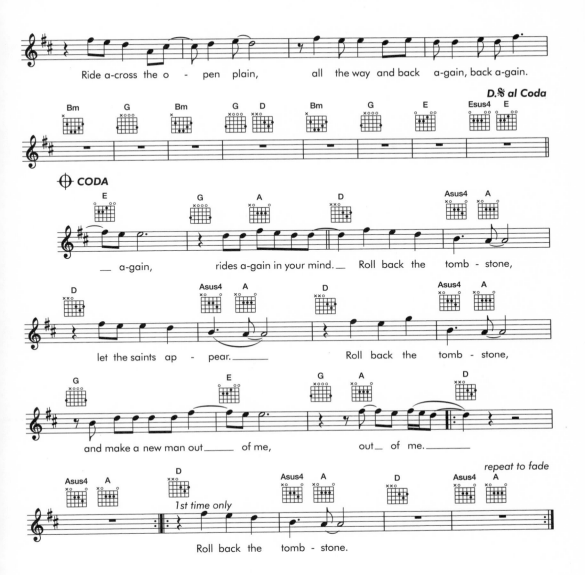

Ride a-cross the o - pen plain, all the way and back a-gain, back a-gain.

D.℠ al Coda

Bm G Bm G D Bm G E Esus4 E

✛ **CODA**

E G A D Asus4 A

_ a-gain, rides a-gain in your mind._ Roll back the tomb - stone,

D Asus4 A D Asus4 A

let the saints ap - pear._ Roll back the tomb - stone,

G E G A D

and make a new man out_ of me, out_ of me._

repeat to fade

Asus4 A D Asus4 A D Asus4 A

1st time only

Roll back the tomb - stone.

Beware of the passenger
The train already left the station
We are neither at home nor at work
We are moving

Listen to the howling of steel
A face betraying no emotion
Like you never had a chance to be
Wild and free

Roll back the tombstone
Let the saints appear
Roll back the tombstone
Till the Lone Ranger rides again
Rides again in your mind
Ride across the open plain
All the way and back again, back again

Listen to the howling of steel
A face betraying no emotion
Like you never had a chance to be
Wild and free

Roll back the tombstone
Let the saints appear
Roll back the tombstone
Till the Lone Ranger rides again
Rides again in your mind

48 Walking On The Spot

Words and Music by Neil Finn

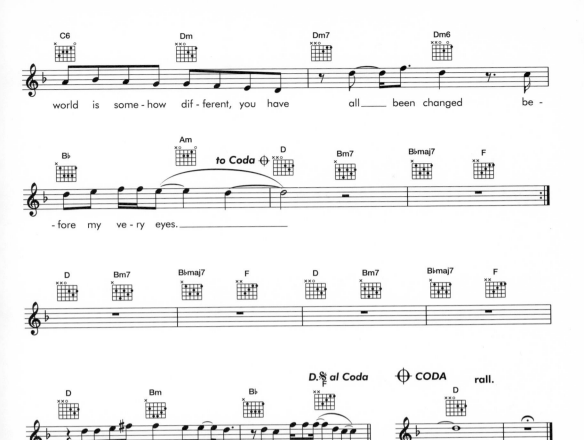

world is some-how dif-ferent, you have all___ been changed be-

-fore my ve-ry eyes.___

Dish-es are un-washed and bro-ken, all you do is cry.___

Walk around your home
And pour yourself a drink
Fire one more torpedo baby
Watch the kitchen sink
Lounging on the sofa maybe
See the living room die
Dishes are unwashed and broken
All you do is cry

Will we be in our minds
When the dawn breaks?
Can we look the milkman in the eye?
The world is somehow different
You have all been changed
Before my very eyes

Dishes are unwashed and broken
All you do is cry

Will we be in our minds
When the dawn breaks?
Can we look the milkman in the eye?
The world is somehow different
You have all been changed
Before my very eyes

49 Weather With You

Words and Music by Neil Finn and Tim Finn

Well, there's a small boat made of china
It's going nowhere on the mantlepiece
Well, do I lie like a loungeroom lizard
Or do I sing like a bird released

Everywhere you go
Always take the weather with you
Everywhere you go
Always take the weather

Everywhere you go
Always take the weather with you
Everywhere you go
Always take the weather, the weather with you

50 When You Come

Words and Music by Neil Finn

When you come_ a-cross the sea,
me like a bea-con guid - ing you to safe-ty,_____ the
soon-er the bet-ter now._ And when you_ come_ the hills will breathe,
like a ba - by pulled up heav - ing from the bot-tom of the o - cean,____
_____ the soon-er the bet-ter_ now._ And when you_ come
____ to co-ver me with your kis - ses fresh____ like a dai-sy chained
____ up in a li-on's den,_____ the soon-er the bet-ter_ now.
I'll know you by____ the thun-der-clap, pour-ing like a rain of blood to my e-mo-tions.
And that is why____ I stum-ble to_ my knees,

in - to my____ ho - ri - zon____ like a cu-mu-lo - nim - bus

com-ing in__ from a dis - tance,____ burn-ing and ex - plod - ing,____

__ burn - ing and ex - plod - ing____ like a slow__ vol - ca - no,

when you come._____ When you come,____

co-ver the ground, co-ver the ground____ with ash - es,____

with ash - es.____ Ba-by, when you come,____

when you come,____ when you come.____

And when you come to cover me
With your kisses hard like armour
The sooner the better now

I'll know you by the thunderclap
Pouring like a rain of blood
To my emotions, hey
And that is why I stumble to my knees
And why underneath the heavens
With the stars burning and exploding
I know why I could never let you down

She came out of the water into my horizon
Like a cumulonimbus coming in from a distance
Burning and exploding, burning and exploding
Like a slow volcano, when you come
When you come, cover the ground
Cover the ground with ashes, with ashes
Baby, when you come, when you come

51 Whispers And Moans

Words and Music by Neil Finn

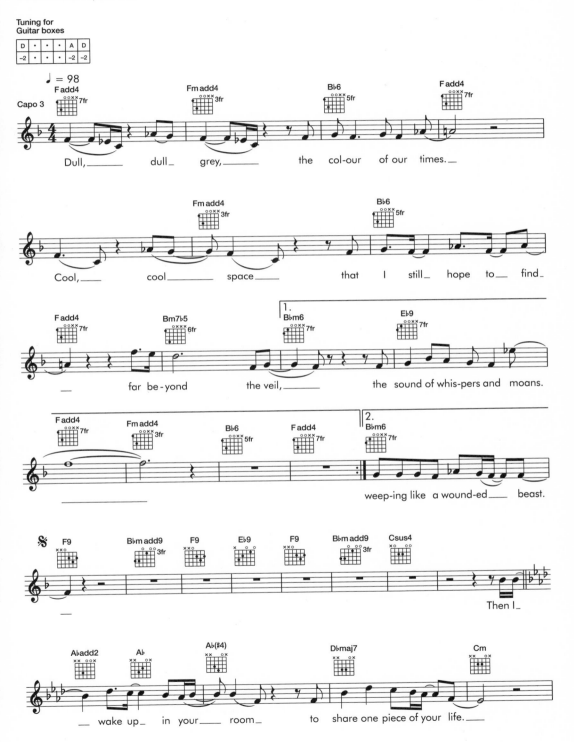

When to-mor-row comes we may not__ be here at all,__ with - out your whis-pers and moans

'cos here you come__ to car-ry me__

home,_____ here you come__ to car-ry me__ home,

to Coda ⊕

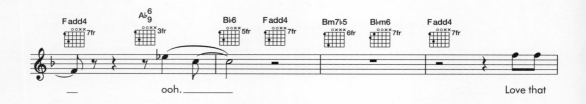

__ ooh._____ Love that

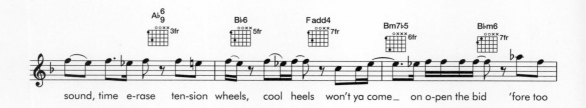

sound, time e-rase ten-sion wheels, cool heels won't ya come__ on o-pen the bid 'fore too

D.%. al Coda

⊕ **CODA**

long._____

We are the mir-rors, are the mir-rors of each

oth-er in a life-time of sus-pi - cion. Cleansed in a mo-ment, a flash of re-cog-ni-tion, you

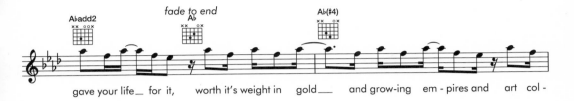

fade to end

gave your life_ for it,   worth it's weight in   gold_   and grow-ing em - pires and   art col -

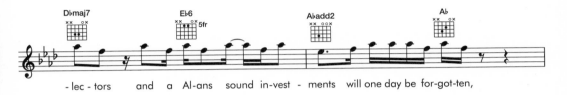

- lec - tors   and a Al-ans   sound in-vest - ments   will one day be for-got-ten,

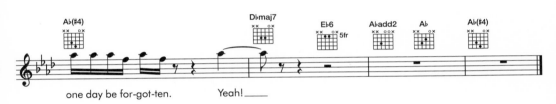

one day be for-got-ten.   Yeah!___

Slow time bomb, the clamour of the street
I hear this town, it never goes to sleep
And I will catch the taxi driver
Weeping like a wounded beast

Then I wake up in your room
Share one piece of your life
When tomorrow comes
We may not be here at all
Without your whispers and moans
Here you come to carry me home
Love that sound, time erase
Tension wheels, cool heels
Won't ya come on open the bid before too long

Then I wake up in your room
Share one piece of your life
I'd give anything to be a fly upon the wall
And hear your whispers and moans
I like to hear your whispers and moans
Here you come to carry me home

We are the mirrors of each other
In a lifetime of suspicion
Cleansed in a moment, a flash of recognition
You gave your life for it
Worth it's weight in gold and growing empires
Art collectors and Alans sound investments
Will one day be forgotten, one day be forgotten
Yeah!

52 World Where You Live

Words and Music by Neil Finn

Here's some-one now_ whose got the mus-cle, his stead-y hand_ could move a moun-tain.

Ex-pert in bed,_____ but come on now, there must be some-thing miss-ing._

That gol-den one_ leads a dou-ble life, you'll find out._ Tell me, I don't

know where you go,_____ do you climb in-to space,_____

_ to the world where you live,_____ to the world where you live?

Oh_ ooh._ Oh_ oh.

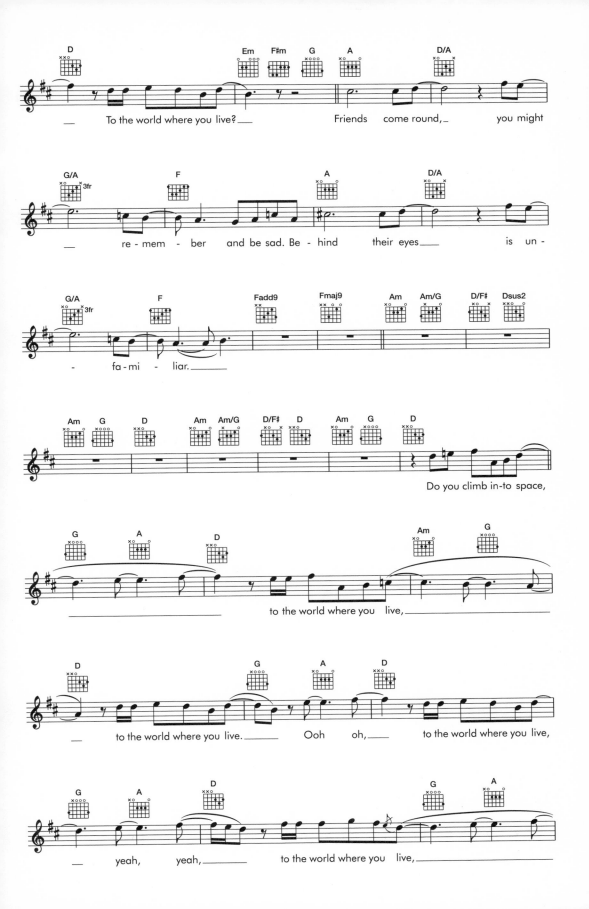

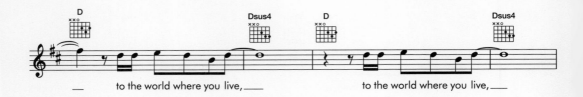

to the world where you live, ___   to the world where you live, ___

to the world where you   live? _____

So here we lie against each other
These four walls can never hold us
We're looking for wide open spaces
High above the kitchen
And we're strangers here
On our way to some other place

But I don't know where you go
Do you climb into space
To the world where you live
The world where you live
Oh, oh to the world where you live?

Friends come round
You might remember and be sad
Behind their eyes is unfamiliar

Do you climb into space
To the world where you live
The world where you live, oh
To the world where you live?

the INDEX

INDEX